# DESTINY CALLS

# DESTINY CALLS
## LIVING YOUR DREAM

## NORMAN & GRACE BARNES

**Canaan**Press

**Canaan**Press

Copyright © 2009 – Norman Barnes and Grace Barnes

First published in Great Britain by Canaan Press in 2009

**Canaan Press**
PO Box 3070
Littlehampton
West Sussex
BN17 6WX
office@canaanpress.co.uk
www.canaanpress.co.uk

The book imprint of
**Matt's Canaan Trust**
www.mattscanaantrust.com

British Library Cataloguing in Publication Data
A record of this book is available from the British Library

ISBN: 978-0-9551816-8-9

Designed by Andy Ashdown
www.andyashdowndesign.co.uk

Cover photograph © iStockphoto.com

Manufactured in Malta by Gutenberg Press Limited

# DEDICATION

To all those who have inspired, blessed and
encouraged us – sometimes against all odds –
not to give up, but to press on to finish well.

# ENDORSEMENTS

This book is a dream fulfilled and is still being fulfilled.
*Gerald Coates* – *Founder Pioneer, speaker, author and broadcaster.*

T. E. Lawrence observed, 'Dreamers of the day are dangerous men, for they may act their dream with open eyes, to make it possible.' Norman and Grace Barnes are dreamers of the day – and they have witnessed their dreams, activated by courageous faith, shake and shape nations. Do you feel your dream has died? Christians affirm that we 'believe in the resurrection of the dead'. Not only does God bring people back to life, He can breathe resurrection life into your dream, as well. Often dreams die for a season, so that destiny may live. Read this important book. Dare to dream again, because your *destiny calls*!
*David Shibley* – *President, Global Advance.*

This is a book written from the heart, forged on the anvil of personal experience, laced with disappointment, frustration and misunderstanding that all true visionaries must endure. It encourages ordinary people who may have forgotten how to dream and how to believe God, to dust themselves down and dare to dream again. I have known Norman and Grace as close friends for 18 years. This is the real deal.
*Rich Hubbard* – *CEO, Links International and part of the leadership team of Arun Community Church, Littlehampton, England.*

God has always used dreamers to effect significant change. Norman and Grace are dreamers, and in this book they describe how God put dreams into their hearts and what that has led to.

Amid the immense joy of seeing dreams fulfilled, prayers answered, amazing supernatural encounters and the miraculous, dreaming can also involve intense pain, suffering, bitter blows, harsh disappointments and unanswered questions.

Norman and Grace tell their story, written in a natural, chatty style that reflects their personalities. They tell of their dreams to be involved in overseas mission, to see miracles, to have children; of the opportunities that opened up for them in America, then India, China and Thailand. They use their vast experiences to inspire and challenge others. The book is real – it tracks the lows as well as the highs – but it imparts vibrant, dynamic faith.

Like the owner of the house that Jesus refers to, as good teachers they are able to bring both new and old out of the storeroom. Their dreaming and vision continue, their fire and passion remain undiminished, though like Abraham, some things they will only see and welcome from a distance.

Through this book, Norman and Grace encourage other ordinary Christians to embrace the dreams that God has put in their hearts, and through patience and perseverance, reach their destiny.

**David Thatcher** – *Pastor, Arun Community Church, Littlehampton.*

Norman is the real deal, he doesn't just 'talk it' but he 'walks it'. When I'm around Norman I feel I can do more, become more and dream for greater things than I would normally live for. He is a true father and I'm proud to be one of his sons. Read and be inspired.

**Martin Smith** – *Delirious?*

*Destiny Calls* is a much needed book that links world vision with access points for ordinary people. Dreaming for the Kingdom is a dangerous but fulfilling occupation. Norman and Grace prove that if you stick around long enough you can walk right into your dreams. This is an honest, humorous and faith-building book.

**Stuart Bell** – *Senior Pastor of New Life Church, Lincoln and founder/leader of Ground Level Network.*

This book is the personal story of Norman and Grace Barnes which challenges you to overcome the disappointments of life and fulfil your destiny. It looks at betrayal, disappointment and even childlessness, and encourages you to hold fast to your dreams and win. An easy read which will give you hope!

**Rachel Hickson** – *author of 'Supernatural Communication – The Privilege of Prayer' and 'Supernatural Breakthrough – a Heartcry for Change'.*

'Tell me your dreams and I will tell you your future.' Those words began to radically change the course of my life several years ago. One of the primary activities of the Holy Spirit in the life of an individual is to awaken them to the God of possibilities within them, and in this book, my friend Norman Barnes is the 'alarm clock' to get you moving. From his own personal journey, the insights he shares will stir anyone to enlarge their perspective and believe for the impossible. This is not a book of theory, but rather proven principles that will allow you to live your life beyond yourself. Enjoy!

**Bishop Tony Miller** – *Senior Pastor, Cathedral of Praise, Oklahoma City, Oklahoma, USA and founder of Destiny Outreach Ministries.*

I once heard someone say, 'Attempt something so impossible that unless the Lord intervenes you will not be able to do it!'. In the years we have had the honour of working with Grace and Norman Barnes, we have seen them conduct their lives and ministry in just this fashion. This book *Destiny Calls* has the potential to change your life. I believe it will challenge you to dream again!

**David Meyer** – *CEO, Hand of Hope, Joyce Meyer Ministries.*

I have known Norman Barnes for 45 years since we first met when he was just 17 years old and he has not changed one little bit! He is still the same fiery, enthusiastic and determined person he was back then in 1963, the only difference is that he has almost half a century of experience of trusting and proving God behind him. He was, and still is, a great dreamer and is just the one to encourage others to dream their dreams and to inspire faith in them to see their dreams become a reality. I was delighted to serve Norman and Grace as chairman of Links International for more than 20 years and can therefore heartily commend *Destiny Calls* to all would-be dreamers and pioneers!

**John Noble** – *Pioneer Network of Churches and chairman of the National Charismatic Leaders Conference from 1984-2006.*

Norman Barnes writes as he lives. Full of compassion and grace, yet vigorous and determined to see things change. This is not a book to read if you're sitting comfortably, but in an uncomfortable world it comes as a message of hope for those who truly need it most. A must read for 2009.

**Clive Calver** – *Senior Pastor, Walnut Hill Community Church, Connecticut, USA.*

# CONTENTS

Acknowledgements . . . . . . . . . . . . . . . . . . . . . . . . . . . . . . . . 10

Foreword. . . . . . . . . . . . . . . . . . . . . . . . . . . . . . . . . . . . . . . . . 11

Prologue . . . . . . . . . . . . . . . . . . . . . . . . . . . . . . . . . . . . . . . . 13

1  Dreams can make you dangerous . . . . . . . . . . . . . . . . . . . . 17

2  The dream in Grace's heart. . . . . . . . . . . . . . . . . . . . . . . . . 38

3  Dreams, dreams and more dreams . . . . . . . . . . . . . . . . . . . 48

4  In Abraham's footsteps . . . . . . . . . . . . . . . . . . . . . . . . . . . . 56

5  Bring on the good times – and the bad . . . . . . . . . . . . . . . . 64

6  The power and the pain . . . . . . . . . . . . . . . . . . . . . . . . . . . 80

7  Forming Links . . . . . . . . . . . . . . . . . . . . . . . . . . . . . . . . . . 92

8  More than one way to have children. . . . . . . . . . . . . . . . . . 108

9  The land of dreams . . . . . . . . . . . . . . . . . . . . . . . . . . . . . . 122

10  India – frustration and fascination . . . . . . . . . . . . . . . . . . . 132

11  Great walls in China . . . . . . . . . . . . . . . . . . . . . . . . . . . . . 148

12  When God says no . . . . . . . . . . . . . . . . . . . . . . . . . . . . . . 165

13  The last chapter?. . . . . . . . . . . . . . . . . . . . . . . . . . . . . . . . 171

# ACKNOWLEDGEMENTS

This book has been a lifetime in the making and we are so grateful to those who have contributed to the richness of our lives in Christ.

Our thanks to Joyce, who befriended Grace at the age of 11 and who is still her friend to this day. Thanks also go to my sister Ann, who challenged me about faith in Christ when I was 16 – I've never looked back.

There have been many people who have listened to us and supported us in the good times and the difficult ones – to you, we say thank you.

Grace and I would also like to thank Canaan Press for publishing this book, Richard Hubbard and Steve Legg for their expertise and input, Rod Boreham for writing the original text, and the staff at Potential.UK.com for editing it.

# FOREWORD

*He's just a dreamer*

It's not an accolade that many of us would welcome too quickly. It sounds like a photo-fit description of an airhead, someone with their brain in the clouds and their feet in process of vertical take off; a person who squanders their days mulling over fairy-tale notions that will never cause anyone to live happily ever after.

But if that's our view of a dreamer, then we couldn't be more wrong. God has always used dreamers – people who allow their hearts and minds to look beyond the concrete horizon of what is and think big enough to include what just might be – to change the world. The notion of a black American President, or a flattened Berlin Wall – these once were the province of dreamers. True dreamers aren't idle. They add faith to their dreams, and ask God to weed out the superficial stuff of self and fill them with *His* dreams. In our compulsively depressed culture which is so stained with cynicism, we desperately need dreamers who will long for more than 15 minutes of fame, a better car, or an easy life.

And that's why I'm privileged to commend this book. Norman and Grace Barnes, who, like me, are Essex people, have always been dreamers for as long as I've known them – and that is a very long time indeed. As a brand new Christian at the age of 17, I was taken along to leaders' meetings at their home in Chadwell Heath. I knew that I had stumbled upon a dreamers' club – women and men who gathered together and were actually mad enough to believe they could change the world.

Norman and Grace don't just talk dreams – they've lived them, often through some nightmare experiences.

And so read this book, but do far more than read – ask God to ignite fresh dreaming in you once more.

**Jeff Lucas**
*Author, speaker and broadcaster*

# PROLOGUE

I'd like to tell you a true story that may shock you. It's one that had a tragic bearing on my family.

I had an older brother called Thomas. But I never knew him. My father killed him in a terrible accident at home. I was just a baby at the time.

Dad worked for Ford in Dagenham, and one day he came home with an automatic Bren rifle. He'd been given the gun as he was serving in the Home Guard, the country's last line of defence against a German invasion.

Thomas, like any inquisitive five-year-old, picked up the weapon and asked, 'What's this, Daddy?'

My father picked up the gun and showed him.

'Shoot me, Daddy, shoot me!' Thomas squealed in excitement.

My father picked it up, and playfully took a 'shot' at Thomas.

He thought the magazine was empty, as it had been cleared at the firing range. But it wasn't. There was one bullet left in the chamber. He squeezed the trigger. That bullet killed Thomas instantly.

I was told my mother screamed for two days with shock and my father was charged with manslaughter. At the inquest, the Coroner said he had been 'very stupid' and recorded a verdict of accidental death. The story made the national papers. I've still got the cutting.

My father never got over this awful tragedy. Who could? He spent decades, tormented with guilt and grief. Every Sunday morning, Dad used to take me on the crossbar of his bike to tend little Thomas' grave. When I got older I discovered who Thomas was, and how he died.

Dad turned to drink and became very depressed. One night he came home dreadfully drunk – he'd consumed around 14 pints of beer.

My mum said she'd leave him if he did it again, and by sheer will power, he never drank again for many years.

Eventually, both he and my mum got saved, and God brought a lot of healing to them. Dad never went to visit the grave again. But he still suffered from terrible depression.

Years later, when I was Pastor of the Chadwell Christian Mission on the outskirts of East London, he came to a meeting. A guy named Dave Mansell was speaking. Dave was well known for hearing clearly from God about people's lives and situations.

He'd never met my dad before and knew nothing about him. But during the meeting, he looked straight at him and said, 'Sir, God knows how you feel. He killed His Son, too.'

This penetrating word of love brought healing to my tormented dad. His depression miraculously lifted and he spent many years living in relative peace before he went to be with the Lord – and Thomas – in 1998.

What has this got to do with a book about fulfilling your destiny? Everything.

In the Bible, exciting dreams and desperate pain go together. You don't often find one without the other.

Grace and I have found that being God's dreamers involves exhilarating highs ... and some cruel and demoralising lows. Prayers aren't answered. God says no. Friends let you down. Plans go wrong. As my dad found, life can deal you some blows that are just too terrible to cope with.

Some people let things like this destroy them – and who can blame them? They believe God can never use them – that they're disqualified.

But my dad's story shows that God is deeply and personally involved with every aspect of our suffering. There's no sin He cannot forgive, no situation that He cannot use to produce good, no problem that's too grave for Him to solve.

If you're feeling disqualified from dreaming great dreams, then you are probably more qualified than most people. God uses failures and rejects to establish His Kingdom.

If you bought this book to get a Quick Fix to the Promised Land of Candyfloss Callings and Doughnut Dreams, you may need to ask for your money back!

*Destiny Calls* is for ordinary people. People like Grace and I, who have more questions than answers, who struggle to cope with the way life has worked out, and who perhaps carry deep pain ... but who decide to give it a go anyway, to dream God's dreams and try to work with Him and make them happen.

You're unique. You carry a unique dream in your heart. You're not disqualified – no one is.

God killed His Son for you, to confirm it.

**Norman and Grace Barnes**
*Rustington, January 2009*

# CHAPTER 1

# DREAMS CAN MAKE YOU DANGEROUS

### Back to the future

I began to shake and tears ran down my face, onto my sweat-stained shirt.

I just couldn't grasp what was happening … in front of me, 5,000 Ghanaians were raising their hands, singing, clapping, shouting and dancing before their God.

Then I was preaching … and hordes of black faces were running towards the platform, eager to make friends with Jesus. My tears carried on flowing as I prayed for them. The occasion was almost surreal … it was as if I'd seen it before.

And I had. I'd dreamt about it, 20 years earlier …

### Dreaming God's dreams

Do you dream? Not just while you're asleep … do you dream about a better tomorrow? Do you nurture hopes, desires and ambitions?

Most people dream about something – whether it's buying a new car, getting a promotion or asking someone out on a date. Everyone longs for something better – that's why we make New Year resolutions.

God dreams, too. He dreams about you and your tomorrows. His message throughout history has been, 'The best is yet to come.' And it still is.

Life can be boring and mundane if you don't have dreams. There's nothing more soul-destroying than working away without the hope of personal fulfilment.

Dreamers are often frowned upon in our culture. People say they have their heads in the clouds, rather than getting on with the here and now. We've all met individuals like that. And to be fair, some dreamers do need to wake up a bit! But life's tough without dreams.

People are dreaming a lot right now. Why? Because society is fragmenting, the economy is collapsing and people are hurting. They are longing for a different day. That's why they turn to drugs, the occult and other religions. That's why they elected a dreamer to be president of the USA. They're craving for hope.

But Christians should be the people to introduce them to the God who is hope itself.

## In the beginning ...

Whenever something significant is achieved, someone, somewhere, dreamt about it first ... whether it is an architect working on a revolutionary design, a scientist searching for a cure for a killer disease, a married couple longing for a family, a man landing on the moon, or missionaries setting up schools, hospitals and churches in far off places.

Many of our personal achievements and landmarks begin as seeds of thought that gradually grow and fill our hearts and minds. Eventually they become visions worth pursuing, goals to strive for … and maybe even to die for.

Tragically, some people's dreams are selfish, evil even, and would be better left unfulfilled. Hitler had a dream that produced the most terrible and tragic carnage across the world.

We all have dreams that have been placed in our hearts by a loving Father. And He wants us to grasp them and join Him in making them come true.

It's easier said than done, though. Sadly, churches are sometimes responsible for crushing people's dreams, rather than nurturing them. That's why you find disillusioned people in churches – both 'new', and denominational. They had a dream – but didn't have an opportunity to fulfil it. Maybe their dream was ridiculed. Maybe it threatened the status quo. Maybe it made the leader feel insecure. Or maybe it was a calling to the 'world' – and people labelled it as 'worldly'. Dreams die for all kinds of reasons. And people can die with them. How will you work out your dream in your church?

When people's dreams hit an obstacle, most of them quit – but some look for a different way to fulfil them. Many 'para-church' organisations and missionary societies evolved because churches couldn't cope with their founders' visions. God has shown throughout history that if the Church won't join what He's doing, then He'll bypass it and start something else!

## Caution – dreamers at work

Dreamers are dangerous because they're prepared to live and die for their dream. And Satan will do everything he can to stop them – dreamers terrify him. He tried to wipe out one dream-filled baby named Moses, and another named Jesus … and he'll try it with you. He opposes anyone with a dream. You need to be vigilant.

Maybe the enemy has wiped your dream out already. But don't be discouraged – and don't give up! Remember what Joseph told his brothers after it appeared they had destroyed his destiny. 'You intended to harm me, but God intended it for good.' Maybe you can't see how God can possibly restore your broken dreams right now. But that doesn't matter. He'll do it anyway if you can hang in there and keep your attitudes right.

Churches are great places for pastors and prophets to dream – they have the people, the time, the money and the facilities to help those dreams come true. But what do our churches do to help the businessmen, the teachers, the political activists and the farmers to fulfil their dreams? Very little – if anything.

That's because 'dreaming' churches are dangerous places. People who dream about making their mark on the world are very difficult to control. They're hard to understand. They don't always fit in. Many leaders are keener on building churches than establishing God's Kingdom. Churches are more controllable, easier to visualise and easier to contain.

In contrast, establishing God's Kingdom is risky. It doesn't have walls, buildings or barriers. It's established wherever God's dreamers have the faith, the love and the supernatural power to make a difference. That could be in the pub, in the Stock Exchange, in the gutter or in Starbucks. It takes a brave pastor to send a businessman or businesswoman to fulfil a vision in the city. He'd sooner have them – and their tithes – at the prayer meeting. How sad.

Please don't think I'm knocking the Church! God has used the Church to establish His Kingdom since the book of Acts. The Church is His Plan A – and He doesn't have a Plan B. But the

Church should be the people who help dreamers possess their tomorrows – not hinder them.

## You're unique

I'm really excited that science now confirms what the Bible has stated for centuries – that *you* are unique. Psalm 139 says you are fearfully and wonderfully made. David wrote that thousands of years ago – and now science is slowly catching up.

Fingerprints have confirmed your unique identity for a long time. But now DNA and eye recognition endorse it, too. You are different to everyone else – right down to the minutest cell in your body.

Twins may share the same DNA, but they have different fingerprints! So they're unique, too! I bet the police department is relieved.

Some Christians are slow to recognise how significant this is. If you are unique, then God must have a unique dream for you. He has a plan, a dream or a mission, hard-wired into your DNA. And if you don't fulfil it, it won't get done. Jeremiah 1 confirms this. God told the young prophet, 'Before I formed you in the womb, I knew you, before you were born I set you apart; I appointed you as a prophet to the nations.' *You* were set apart for a special task before you were born. And no one's disqualified.

Imagine what would happen if we all grasped this. We'd unleash an explosion of spiritual change that would shake every nation on earth. It's been done before. Look what Bible dreamers like Joseph and Paul did when they understood their unique destinies. With God, they produced changes that crossed national borders and altered history.

Imagine Joseph and Paul – multiplied by a million! That's what we could achieve together.

I meet a lot of people who've had dreams hidden in their hearts for years, but they became discouraged because nothing happened. Others found those dreams were overtaken by the demands of family, home, work and church. Some saw their dreams shattered by traumatic or dramatic experiences.

But I can confidently tell these people, 'God is in the business of restoring your broken dreams and fulfilling hearts' desires. He can make dreams into a living reality.'

It's never too late!

### I had a dream …

My heart's always been full of things I'd love to see. So has Grace's. And we have tried our best to pursue them … sometimes with mixed results!

I became a Christian when I was 16, and God put a vision in my heart to help people in other countries, almost from the start.

Grace and I belonged to a youth group at Dagenham Elim Church, and the Holy Spirit was doing some special things there back in the late 1950s. Sometimes God's presence filled the room in such a tangible way, that we found ourselves prostrated on the floor. This phenomenon is now called 'being slain in the Spirit' and is still controversial. But back in 1958, we didn't care what it was called. We were young, full of expectancy and had a burning desire to serve God and to know His power.

On one occasion, the Holy Spirit touched me when I was praying in one of our youth group meetings. My knees buckled and I fell on my face before the Lord. I spoke in tongues for around two hours, and as I did so, I saw a vision that was so real, I could have touched it.

I felt as if I had been transported to another country. I could see myself preaching from an elevated platform in a large building. The words I was uttering in tongues corresponded with what I heard myself preaching. As I moved around the platform, I saw a sea of black faces listening intently. Many of them streamed forward to meet with God when I gave an appeal at the end ...

... and then the vision faded.

I was excited, and deeply moved. I knew I had 'seen' somewhere in Africa. And as I 'came round', I looked at the 20 other young people in the room in bewilderment.

'Have I been here all the time?' I asked them.

'Yes, of course you have,' they assured me, slightly puzzled.

I explained what had happened. And then, full of youthful self-confidence, I boldly declared, 'One day, God will get me to Africa.' The looks on my friends' faces showed they were not as confident about it as I was! But Charles Calvert, the leader, took me to one side and said, 'You believe it, Norman. One day God will get you there.' That was a real encouragement.

Looking back, it must have seemed ludicrous to everyone else. Who did this young lad from Dagenham, Essex, think he was? I was a bit of a loud-mouth, and I must have sounded arrogant. I probably was. But I did have a deep desire to serve God. And I knew I couldn't rest until I saw the dream fulfilled.

Looking back, I should have kept my mouth shut. The Bible talks about people 'pondering things in their hearts'. That's what I should have done. Some people thought I was a big-head. Some still do!

I was like the young Joseph we read about in Genesis. He had dreams – and didn't waste any time telling his jealous brothers about them. And he paid a very harsh price for not engaging his brain before he opened his mouth.

### I want patience – immediately!

I was confident I would serve the Lord full-time and travel the world. But like Joseph, I was impatient. I wanted God to fulfil His promises straight away. I wrestled with Him about it, plagued Him and agonised over it. I desperately wanted to see some action. And eventually, God told me, 'After you have received the promise, wait patiently.' He needed to take me through some tough times to develop my character, so I could be trusted with His dreams.

You only have to watch TV to see what happens to people with great dreams but no character … the lives of people like George Best, Britney Spears and Amy Winehouse shout their own tragic message. We should learn from their mistakes.

### Why the ceiling on healing?

During my travels as a young man, I often spent time with a man named Les Hilary. When he broke bread, he said, 'Thank You, Lord, for another week of perfect health.'

Les was a great example of divine health and I was challenged by his attitude. So I began to seek God about healing. I began to realise that the Gospel should be demonstrated with signs and wonders, so people would know that God really is their Lord. Paul told the church in Corinth, 'I didn't come to you with words, but power.' To Grace and I, that's how it should be. Miracles were important to Jesus. They didn't just meet people's needs – they also proved who He was. That's why the disciples put their faith in Him after He turned water into wine at Cana. And I suspect they enjoyed the wine, too!

Miracles were part of Jesus' life, and part of the lives of Peter, Philip, Paul and other disciples in the early church. So why weren't they part of my life, and the lives of people working with me? Grace and I longed to see God's healing power, so that people would sit up and take notice. We were grateful for the isolated miracles we saw. But we were convinced that regular, abundant miracles should be the norm – and not just for Norm, but for the whole Church! We found ourselves moved at the sight of suffering. Seeing someone in a wheelchair made us cry.

I read every book I could find on healing and prayed constantly for a healing ministry. And I was never afraid to take risks, even though I sometimes acted with presumption rather than in faith. I started to pray for sick people in the street. Once, I was preaching on a soap-box outside Foyle's bookshop in London, and declared with utter confidence, 'God is a God of miracles.'

'Do you really believe that?' a man in the crowd shouted back at me.

'Yes,' I replied, still full of youthful confidence.

'Do you believe God can heal?' the man persisted.

'Yes, I do.'

'Do you think God can heal this?' he asked, and held up his hand.

The man's hand was paralysed – it was like a claw. The joints in his hand were stuck rigid. Apparently the hospital had written to him saying there was nothing they could do for him.

I got down from my soap-box and made my way through the crowd to him. I asked God to heal him and the power of the Holy Spirit touched him. He moved his fingers and began jumping up and down with excitement, telling everyone what had happened.

The crowd doubled. People came running. I was thrilled – it confirmed that God wanted to accompany preaching with signs and wonders.

Another time, Doug Barnett, of the Saltmine Trust, asked Grace and me if we would look after the people at Spring Harvest who were marginalised. There were some people who were afraid of big crowds, or had other difficulties. 'We'd love to!' I told him. 'But can we do it our way?'

'Yes, of course,' said Doug. I suspect he wondered what he was letting himself in for! But God did some wonderful miracles that week. There was a lad of around 20 who was confined to a wheelchair, but when we prayed for him, he got up and walked! As far as I know, he's still walking now.

Grace had a similar experience at a women's conference in Goodmayes. A woman who had irons on both legs asked for prayer. As Grace prayed, the woman's legs clicked back into place and when she got home, she took off the irons and walked normally! Later, she gave her testimony – and danced, to prove what God had done.

Then in April 2008, we visited Riverside Church in Nottingham, and chatted to a couple who had a lovely little girl, who was aged around three. But she was clearly unhappy. I asked her what was wrong and her dad told me that she was going into hospital to have a lump removed from her neck.

I asked her if I could pray for her. 'No!' she said, with all the frankness of a three-year-old. But her dad persuaded her. And he emailed us three weeks later saying the lump had gone and the doctors had confirmed that some glands, which had been affected by the growth, were working normally.

## A vision – about having better vision!

One thing bothered me. I was preaching about God's healing power – but I had worn glasses with very strong lenses since my school days. My sight was so poor that when I had an eye test, I couldn't even see the top line of the card!

I prayed for healing many times, removed my glasses ... but nothing happened. There was a contradiction between my beliefs and my experience. It didn't make sense.

One evening Grace and I were listening to our dear friend, Cecil Cousens, speaking on faith. Once again I prayed about my eyes, and I heard God say, 'Now!' I knew I had to obey immediately. So I removed my glasses and gave them to Grace.

Next morning, a Monday, I woke up and could see perfectly. Up to then, I couldn't see the time on the alarm clock by the bed – a blessing sometimes on a Monday morning! But not as big a blessing as being able to see it!

I walked to work on air, praising God. My colleagues asked where my glasses were. 'God's healed me,' I told them with complete confidence. They tried to explain it away, but they couldn't deny what had happened.

I rejoiced all week because I could see without glasses. But then, on Saturday morning, I woke up – and couldn't see the alarm clock. My sight was as bad as ever. I went shopping with Grace to buy her a new pair of boots, and couldn't even read the price tags (which was probably just as well!). But I refused to put my glasses back on. I walked round the whole weekend saying, 'Lord, if you can do it for one week, you can do it for good. I claim my healing.'

On Monday morning my sight was perfect again, and I didn't wear glasses from the age of 22 to 41. And even then it was just for watching TV and night driving. God had taught me to have faith for healing – and to have faith to keep it, too. It was an important lesson.

Inevitably, I became a real pain to anyone who wore glasses. I urged them to seek God for healing. I was insensitive and had to learn the hard way that things were not always that simple.

But my healing gave me faith for other people with sight problems. Once, while we were in India, we prayed for a woman who was partially blind. She couldn't even see the six inch letters on the posters on the wall. But after we prayed for her, she went to the back of the hall and read the text fluently. And it was a long hall! She could still see when we went back the following year.

### We're sick of sickness

Grace and I still dream about seeing greater healings, and seeing them more often. We've never believed God wants His children sick, and we still don't. We started dreaming about it more than 40 years ago … and we're still longing for it today!

During a trip to America in 1985, a minister told us that God would soon begin to fulfil our hearts' desires about healing. But God's idea of 'soon' wasn't the same as ours. We're still waiting.

Looking back, I can see the reasons for the delay. I couldn't have been trusted with a big healing ministry. I would have been proud, unbearable – and I had to learn many lessons first.

### When God doesn't deliver

So there we were, longing for healings and yearning to go to Africa. But nothing was happening. By then we were leading Chadwell Christian Mission on the outskirts of London, but…

It's easy to get down-hearted when God's promises do not materialise as quickly as you'd like. But fortunately Grace and I realised we needed to get on with life. In any case, the desire to serve God was too strong for us to wait around doing nothing.

We joined an evangelistic group called the Good News Team and were inspired by David Wilkerson's book *The Cross and the Switchblade*. So we began helping the drug addicts in Soho and saw some wonderful miracles as God set people free from the power of heroin and other substances. The work was documented in a book by Keith Bill called *The Needle, the Pill and the Saviour.*

From that time we diverted all our energies into every ministry opportunity that came our way. At weekends, we preached in the open air, and in the summer we went to the beach and often saw people weeping as we told the crowds about God's love. It was a great thrill to lead many people to Jesus.

But our emotions see-sawed whenever we thought about that vision of Africa. Sometimes, we were daunted by it. On other occasions, we were frustrated and wondered if God's promises were ever going to be fulfilled. Time was marching on. I was getting older and nothing was happening. In hindsight, we recognise we had to wait for God's moment and learn those tough lessons of patience and perseverance. We carried on hoping, when there was no reason to hope.

### Stepping into my dream

Early in 1979 we received a letter from Ghana from a man called Nicholas Andoh. He'd been given our names by a lady in Germany who had heard me speak. She told him he should contact me if he was ever in need. I'm not sure why – we didn't know anything about his work and had never heard of him, or the lady! He asked for our help – it sounded as if he needed money.

My yearning to go to Africa was stronger than ever – but when the call came, I didn't feel any great desire to respond. We decided to discuss it with our two friends, John Noble and Maurice Smith, who led a church nearby. They suggested I should write back and be non-committal. Wise advice.

Then we received another letter from Nicholas. He told me he had planted three churches and wanted me to preach and to see what God was doing. I decided to speak to Maurice and John again.

'But nobody knows who this man is,' said John. 'I would advise caution, Norman. It could be a confidence trick.'

Maurice thought the opposite. 'We have restrained evangelists long enough,' he said. 'Let this one flap his wings.'

Both opinions sounded wise – I couldn't decide what to do! So we agreed to ask God to confirm his 'call' by providing the money for my fare.

I went home and prayed about it with Grace. And within six weeks we had been given £1,200 – enough to pay for the trip. It comprised different amounts from a variety of sources and was the largest gift we'd ever received. I reported back to John and Maurice. 'Go for it,' they said.

So I wrote to tell Nicholas I was coming to Ghana. The address he had given me was a PO Box number, which turned out to be a sports stadium 180 miles from the capital, Accra. I had no idea if my letter would reach him. To make it worse, the Ghanaian Government had closed the borders during a currency change-over. No planes were entering or leaving – and neither was the post.

While I was making final preparations, I decided to speak to a missionary couple from Ghana who were on furlough in Britain.

They were cautious too. 'You don't even know this man,' they said. They feared that I could find myself in real difficulty, so they gave me the address of a couple called David and Margaret Mills, some Elim Missionaries in Ghana. 'If you are in a fix, they will help you,' they said.

Grace and I agreed I should go ahead, and I booked the tickets, had the injections and obtained a visa. And when the border controls seemed to be relaxing, I sent a cable to the PO Box number, saying when I would arrive – and took the first plane to Accra.

On the plane, however, I discovered the borders hadn't opened after all, and we would have to land in neighbouring Togo. I was worried. Here I was, heading half-way round the world to meet a man I didn't know – and now I wasn't even going to land in the right place! Had Nicholas received my cable? Did he know I was on my way? And if he did, would he turn up a day early and give up when I didn't arrive? But it was too late to turn back. I had to trust the Lord and see what happened.

## Culture shock

The aircraft landed at Lome Airport, Togo, at 6pm. That vision of Africa still burned in my heart … but nothing prepared me for what happened next. It was so hot I thought the plane's engines were still running. Then I realised it was the weather – it was around 40 degrees! I walked across the tarmac in the melting heat, carrying my own bags and being jostled by people rushing to get to the airline office first. There were gun-toting soldiers everywhere, watching the passengers carefully. The contrast between Heathrow and Lome couldn't have been more marked.

The airline, KLM, had arranged for us to stay overnight in a five star hotel. As I joined the queue in the office, I noticed a man standing behind me. He was the only other European on the flight.

'Could I share a room with you?' he asked. He looked as if he knew the ropes. 'Yes, that's fine with me,' I replied. He told me his name was Jim. We checked into the hotel and he suggested we have a meal.

'What do you do for a living?' I asked as we sat down to eat.

'I sell books,' he replied.

'What sort of books?'

'Christian books.'

'Are you a Christian then?' I asked, scarcely able to hide my delight. He was.

'So am I'. And at that moment God spoke to me, right in the midst of my fears and confusion. 'Do not worry, son, I'm with you,' He said.

I got on well with Jim and told him about Nicholas. He offered to help if things didn't work out.

The following day we took off from Lome and were the first plane-load of people to arrive in Accra for a month. It was chaos. There was another mad rush to the airport buildings. No one queued for anything – instead, they bribed officials to get priority treatment. Everything moved so slowly and I grew very impatient. They checked my documents three times, but eventually I got through customs and into the arrival lounge. I'd made it! But it was Tuesday. I should have arrived the day before. Would anyone be there to meet me?

I scanned the building, looking at every face, even though I had no idea what Nicholas looked like. There weren't many white men around, though, so there was a good chance Nicholas would find me – if he was there.

Suddenly someone asked, 'Are you Pastor Barnes?'

'Yes.'

'My name is Nicholas.' I was very relieved to discover he actually existed! After one last word with Jim, I followed Nicholas out of the airport, harassed by the crowds of people who wanted to carry my cases.

I found out later that Nicholas had been praying the day I was due to arrive. He didn't know about my plans, but as he prayed, God told him to go and check his post-box.

'But, Lord,' he protested, 'there hasn't been any mail for weeks.'

But he obeyed – and there in the post-box was the cable telling him when I would arrive. It had miraculously got through – even though the borders were closed. So Nicholas borrowed some money and hitch-hiked to Accra, arriving Monday night. When he wasn't able to find me, he waited until the following morning. So God synchronised our diaries.

The sights, sounds and smells of Accra nearly overwhelmed me as we made our way to the booking office to buy bus tickets to Nicholas' home in Kumasi. There were people everywhere, milling around, shouting and laughing. Everyone seemed friendly. Noisy traders were selling everything from shampoo and vegetables to sweets and hard-boiled eggs. It was good-natured pandemonium!

Up to then, I had only seen people carrying objects on their heads in films. But now I saw it for real – and I was fascinated. And looking around, there were plenty of Christian influences … though not what I'd expected. There were ramshackle shops with names like *God's Love Car Spares* and *Jesus Saves Sewing Machines.* Not what I was used to in Chadwell Heath!

The cracked and broken road outside was bedlam. Orange-and-blue Datsun taxis honked their horns at the small, broken-down mini-buses that were used for local public transport. Everyone was shouting at everyone else. The open sewers were a shock to encounter; so was the broken-down shed that acted as the booking office – and to cap it all, the bus had no springs.

Everyone's luggage was thrown onto the top, along with the goats and chickens. Undeterred, we climbed aboard and made our way to the back seat. As the bus moved off, I sat, my knees tucked under my chin, with red dust blowing in all over me, wondering what on earth I was doing there! The jolting, jarring journey was an experience I never forgot. It was made all the more memorable when a woman held her baby out of the window to urinate while the bus bumped its way down the road.

## Blessed by the poor

After a long, tiring journey, we arrived in Kumasi. I was very hungry – I'd only eaten a banana since I arrived in Ghana. Nicholas, his wife and two children lived in a two-roomed apartment in a run-down tenement block. The conditions, frankly, were terrible. They had very little furniture and no bathroom or toilet. The one toilet along the corridor belonged to the landlord, but I was allowed to use it, because I was a white man. However, it hadn't worked for six months. I'll leave you to guess what it was like.

The family cooked in a community kitchen in a quadrangle outside, and over the next few days I ate everything I was given – meals that would have filled most Europeans with horror.

Nicholas' wife and two children slept in the basement because it was considered unsuitable for a white man. I slept in a bed in one room and Nicholas slept on a cement floor in the other. This poverty-stricken family lived in abominable conditions, but they gave their best to this man from England. I was deeply moved – and appreciated how comfortable life was back home.

It was an eye-opener to travel with Nicholas and see what was happening in his three churches. Preaching there was unlike anything I'd experienced before. English congregations usually sit listening in silence. In Africa, they jump up and down and make far more noise than the preacher!

I asked Nicholas if we could visit David and Margaret Mills, the couple I'd been told about before I left home. So we pushed our way into yet another Datsun four seater taxi, and joined seven people who were already crammed inside. As we drove, I had to hang on to the door to stop it falling off! But we reached the lorry park safely and then climbed aboard a lorry along with the now familiar goats and chickens who were our fellow travellers.

David and Margaret Mills' home was luxurious by Ghanaian standards. And although we had never met before, David and I clicked immediately and became firm friends. I felt like Father Christmas as I handed round some small gifts. I was moved by the enthusiastic response to these relatively insignificant presents.

David asked me to stay with them, but I wanted to honour my promise to spend two weeks with Nicholas. I returned to preach at a church in Kwadaso, a suburb of Kumasi. David must have been impressed, as he invited me to preach at McKeown Temple in Kumasi on Easter Sunday. By now I had been in Ghana for almost three weeks and I agreed to extend the trip to preach at the service.

The surprise of my life awaited me …

### A dream comes true

I had no idea what McKeown Temple was, how big it was, or even who McKeown was – other than being the man after whom the temple was named.

I could tell the service had started, long before we reached the entrance – we could hear the joyful, infectious singing. The building was packed to the doors. Five thousand people were crammed into a space designed for 3,500 … a sea of radiant black faces, smiling and eager. Many of the women were dressed in colourful traditional costume and the men wore shirts and trousers, all immaculately pressed.

We went through a side entrance, straight onto an elevated platform. But I didn't just enter the building. I also entered a time warp – just as I described at the start of this chapter. I had stepped into my dream.

My arms went all goose-pimply and I started to shake and cry. I was living out an action replay of the vision I had received more than 20 years earlier in that small room in the Elim Church in Dagenham. And I knew what was going to happen next. I felt humbled, moved and overwhelmed by God's goodness. I realised that God's timing had been perfect. Had I gone to Ghana any earlier, I would have been intolerable to live with. God's 'man of faith and power for the hour' would not have made many friends – and probably would have failed.

The sight of 5,000 Ghanaians abandoned in worship is enough to reduce the stiffest upper-lipped Englishman to tears. I was no exception. But I wasn't prepared for the offering!

There were incredible scenes as the 5,000 people in the meeting waited their turn to sing and dance their way to the front to put their money in a bowl that was more than two feet in diameter and about eighteen inches deep. They filled it over and over again with notes. The offering took an hour, and the congregation sang right through. I'd never seen anything like it. I felt they needed to minister to me, not the other way around.

My action replay continued as I preached, and then I found myself walking further into that original dream. People responded and came forward as I gave the challenge. God was fulfilling His word. My dream was becoming a reality. And if God could do this, He could keep the rest of His promises. I couldn't wait to get home and tell Grace! I returned to England, utterly convicted that dreams really do come true.

Grace and I went straight out and bought some items for the Mills household and sent them off by freight. We didn't realise this simple act would develop into something much more significant and that my dream would unfold in astonishing ways.

But it is a long way from Dagenham to Accra ...

# CHAPTER 2

# THE DREAM
# IN GRACE'S HEART

### One vision

It would have been difficult if I enjoyed travelling the globe and Grace preferred staying at home in front of the fire! Our dreams and visions have always been compatible and still are. We fulfil them in different ways, of course, because we are very different people (I'm the quiet one!). But our gifts and characters complement one another, and there's a wonderful synergy when we work together.

When people marry, God unites their dreams and visions. It's hard to be 'one flesh' if you're pulling in opposite directions. And it's sad when you see a husband tearing round the world doing 'God's work', while his angry and disinterested wife is stuck at home because she doesn't share his vision. God never wanted it that way. Perhaps couples who find their visions aren't compatible need to come before God and ask for His help.

### What a woman!

I'm quite loud and extrovert, and many people assume that Grace just tagged along behind while I led a church and established Links International. (The story of Links is told in Chapter 7.) If only they knew! Grace has a significant worldwide ministry in her own right and has seen just as many dreams fulfilled as I have. If that surprises you, that's because she's humbler than I am!

People often say, 'If Grace can do it, so can I.' And she takes that as a huge compliment, as she's the last person you might expect God to use, especially in leadership or on public platforms. But that's if you look at it from a worldly point of view, where 'successful' people are educated, have proper training, and come from the right background.

Our God loves to take 'unqualified' people like Grace and use them to make a powerful imprint on history. Grace had very little education, since her schooling was virtually wiped out by the war. But there's a difference between education and intelligence – and what Grace lacked in one, she more than made up for in the other.

Grace also suffers from dyslexia, so she finds it hard to write and spell. But that hasn't stopped her from travelling to 47 countries, meeting the First Lady of Ghana and speaking to meetings of up to 70,000 people. She's also taken teams of women to places like Mexico, India, Ghana, Sri Lanka and Jamaica.

Grace has a heart to encourage women who don't think they've got anything to contribute, or who are too afraid to step out. She understands how they feel.

She says, 'I always tell people that everyone has a gift – something they can offer. Some women get distressed because they don't have a role in church. But maybe God never intended that. Church leaders should remember that some women are called to the world, not church.

'I also make a point of recruiting women for my overseas teams who don't usually do things or have any kind of public or leadership role. I love to encourage them and try to give them confidence. My first role is to win their hearts, so they trust me. And then I might ask them to tell congregations a bit about themselves. By the end of the trip some of them are giving their testimonies, praying for people and prophesying over them.

'But I never, ever push them. You should never push anyone. Our job is to encourage people, not to push them.'

### Greater love …?

Grace earns the friendship and respect from the women on her teams by caring for them – and that needs some radical love at times! While she was in Ghana she asked co-worker, Jane Lindsell, if her knickers needed washing. Jane's response said it all … 'If the team leader is prepared to wash my knickers, then I'm more than happy to follow her!'

Another time, Grace and some other women went into the jungle to have dinner with some village elders. They wanted to meet this white lady who was doing so much to help their people.

The women were given the usual African meal of rice and meat – and it was served in the usual way too, with cats and other animals jumping across the table.

Grace always instructed her team members to eat whatever was put in front of them while they were in other countries. But one lady turned green when a mangy cat started eating the food off her plate. Grace quietly swapped plates with her – and ate the cat's leftovers herself. That's what I call servanthood!

But Grace is also an easy lady to under-estimate – as any of the women who went on those teams will testify! She is very strict and disciplined – essential if you're going to survive in hostile climates and cultures.

### My number one fan

Grace travelled with me right from the start of my international work. We scarcely discussed whether she should come – it seemed the natural thing to do. And she still travels with me, although at our age it's often just a bus ride using senior citizens' passes! But we do make it further afield at times, going to the USA, Thailand and South Africa.

Grace has always been 100 per cent behind everything I do, and she's happy to release me when I have to go away without her. In fact I suspect that sometimes, she can't get me through the door fast enough! She's always content if she has to stay at home, as she can do things she doesn't normally have time for. Sometimes she gets a little impatient with wives who don't like their husbands doing work for God that involves travelling.

She says, 'I can never understand them. Many men have to travel in the course of their jobs. Why should Christian men be any different? Travel is part and parcel of a leader's job, so wives should accept it. They're selfish! Some leaders' wives complain when their husband is away – and when he's at home, they expect him to pick the kids up from school. But churches don't pay their leaders to do that.

'I'm not like a widow who will never see her husband again. I find it easy to release Norman because I know he's coming back.'

I have to say, she's always wonderful to come back to.

### Strong foundations

God had His hand on Grace, right from the moment she was born. He even chose her name.

Her mum and dad had planned to call her Audrey, but she nearly died at birth. The doctor told her parents, 'It's only by God's grace you've got this child.' So they called her Grace ... a name that turned out to be so appropriate.

She was born in Dagenham and came from very humble beginnings. Her father was a porter in Borough market, and her mother was a religious Anglican. But God put her on his apprenticeship programme when she was very young.

You won't find that programme in any training brochure – and if you did, it wouldn't have many recruits. It was called Servanthood. And the syllabus involved sacrificial giving, unconditional caring and loving the unloved.

As a child, she helped her mother care for her elderly grandparents, and as a teenager, ran errands, helping with the housework and looking after them when they were ill. During the war, she used to go with her mum and dad to church halls where babies and young children were taken after their homes were bombed. She helped to feed them and play with them, often just minutes after their parents had been killed by a bomb ... vital love at a tough time.

Then, when she was 17, she looked after her elderly grandmother, who was too ill to care for herself. Grace, with her mother, nursed her until she died. Those early lessons in servanthood prepared her for the loving work she still does today.

When we went to Chadwell Christian Mission in 1966, I was the 'Pastor', but Grace did much of the pastoral work. She inherited a ladies' group that mainly comprised elderly women, and faithfully did their washing every Monday. Our kitchen looked like a Chinese laundry! And she cooked lunch and other meals for all and sundry. There was always someone popping in for a bite to eat. Both our front door and our fridge door were always open!

## Time to pack

God gave Grace a vision for her life before He started on me. Grace was saved when she was 11 and baptised in the Spirit a couple of years later. She started attending Bethel Church in Dagenham, and made a number of good friends there. They went to a youth prayer meeting and Bible study, and one week a girl named Kathy Lucas had a vision to go to Africa.

Grace was thrilled for her, but felt sad, too. She thought to herself, 'Yes, I can see you doing that ... you can read and write well and you go to a grammar school.' Grace didn't have a very high opinion of herself and couldn't see God using her like that.

One afternoon, she went for a walk in Pondfield Park, Dagenham, and cried out to God, 'What have you got for me? How will you use me?'

God's answer came quickly and clearly as she walked along the path between the trees. 'You will travel the world and live out of a suitcase.' I don't think anyone can doubt that this promise was fulfilled ... she's been doing that ever since! It still amazes us how our dreams harmonised, even before we met.

There's more, though. In 1990, Grace and I went to the Congo and Grace spoke at a women's meeting. Afterwards, someone came up to her and said, 'You remind me of another woman who spoke here.' This woman turned out to be Kathy Lucas, who made it to Africa too, and served God there for 35 years before retiring. Grace was dumbstruck. And you can imagine the smile on God's face as He whispered to Grace, 'I kept My promise.'

He certainly did ... and 50 years on, we're both still travelling the world, living out of suitcases – sometimes alone, usually together. Two can put 10,000 to flight. And we're pretty good with unhelpful airport staff, too!

## Blazing the trail

Eventually, many of the ladies in that original women's group died or were too old to get to meetings. But the church grew and began to attract younger ladies, some with young children. Grace began preaching and quickly became an active speaker on the women's meeting circuit. And when we went to the States, she was exposed to some of the major women speakers there.

She recalls, 'They inspired me to go for a wider ministry, not just to women but to mixed congregations. This was a major breakthrough both for me and the Church. I wanted to model something for other women to follow, both those who were on the leadership team and those who weren't.

'As I started travelling to churches with Norman, I began to meet other women who had leadership potential and I gradually got involved in supporting them and caring for them. Before long, I held our first one-day conference in the south of England. More than 100 women spent the day together and had such a good time that the following year, 200 came for a whole weekend.

'Then we started working in the north and saw hundreds of women gathering in Grimsby for the day. We had speakers like Sandra Howells and Betty Jo Frank from the States to encourage women into their ministries. Today there are many in leadership and ministry as a result of those times together. They were special.'

Grace felt she had completed her job when she organised a national women's meeting in Brentwood, Essex, in March 1990. Coaches arrived from all over the country and more than 2,000 women gathered for an inspiring, supernatural time. Not bad for a woman without an education!

Grace often tells me, 'I could never have imagined all this would happen.' And a lot of other people can't believe it, either. But that's because Grace isn't the pushy, 'NOTICE ME' type. She's never demanded a platform or fought for 'women's rights' in the Church. Her heart has just been to see women released to fulfil their hearts' desires – and if that happens to be in leadership, then so be it.

As she sometimes puts it, 'Yes, of course women should be able to lead – provided they get the job on merit. But once they've got it, they shouldn't moan about the "time of the month"!'

That approach has helped to pioneer women's ministry in the UK and beyond – and is still bearing fruit today.

## A friend of God

There's a board covered with photographs in Grace's kitchen. Almost every morning, Grace gets up and prays over everyone on it.

There are photos of friends, family, people who are backslidden and children born to supposedly 'barren' women. You'll even find the scan of an unborn baby there.

While Grace is shaking the heavens with her prayers, you'll usually find me shaking the pillow with my snores … then she comes in with a nice cup of tea and we read the Bible and pray together. We also read Psalm 91.

Grace's life is one continual prayer. And that friendship with God has produced enough stories to merit a book of their own. But let me tell you about the time when she was helped by an angel.

She was travelling to Sri Lanka with two other women, and they arrived to find civil unrest on the island. The atmosphere was tense among the crowds at the airport, and Grace and her friends resigned themselves to a long, hot wait at customs and passport control.

Suddenly a man appeared out of nowhere, went up to Grace and her companions and told them to follow him – he would show them a quick way out of the airport.

He led them round a corner, through a side door – and disappeared. But waiting at the side door was the man who had arranged to meet them. He'd been waiting at the airport's main entrance, but God told him to meet his visitors round the side …

## Five star treatment

If Grace invites you to dinner, you get the five star treatment. There will be a delicious, lovingly-prepared three course meal with wine, preceded by sherry and aperitifs and followed by coffee and sweets … all presented with a warmth and style that would impress the best hotels. A guy who came for dinner once said, 'I felt like I was the most important person on earth.' That's because Grace knows how to honour people – even if the freezer *is* almost empty! But please don't ring for an invitation …!

## Works of art

Grace has also pioneered the creative arts in churches. When we first started in the mission, anything remotely artistic was labelled as 'worldly', or even 'of the devil'. So Grace had a tough job getting people to overcome their fears and doctrinal hang-ups. But her work grew and we also held creative weekends with other church groups. A lot of the poetry, music and the arts you see in modern churches have their roots in those meetings 40 years ago.

## A lady of love

Grace is loved all over the world. Thousands of men, women and children in every continent have been touched by her love, her kindness – and, at times by her directness. She can say tough things kindly – a great gift. She's my great protector … she gets very angry when people hurt me. 'I'd like to wring their necks,' she tells me when she hears about a situation where I've been badly treated or criticised. But fortunately, she always takes that anger and hurt to God and finds the grace to forgive.

Some leaders' wives are 'bolt-ons' to their husband's ministry. But Grace is different. We're bolted together. That's why Grace is right at the front of this book. Many have benefited from her love and the way God has used her in the prophetic and the miraculous – as you'll see later …

# CHAPTER 3

# DREAMS, DREAMS AND MORE DREAMS

## A wake-up call

The words of Martin Luther King still ring loudly in my ears.

'I have a dream,' he declared to the thousands at the Lincoln Memorial back in August 1963. They had come to hear his vision of a world where black and white people could live in harmony, as equals.

The atmosphere was electric. Every word he spoke was like dynamite.

Time and time again he repeated that phrase which seemed to capture the longings of the crowd. 'I have a dream.' Each time he said it, he went on to voice his vision of the future.

'I have a dream,' he cried. Those around him on the platform could be heard muttering their agreement.

'I have a dream,' he repeated. You could feel the vast crowd responding.

'I have a dream,' he shouted. I was watching on television – and his words gripped me. Much to Grace's surprise, I leapt out of my chair, punched the air with my fists and shouted, 'So have I, so have I!'

Those historic words are etched with sadness now. That great man paid a terrible price for his dream. He lived for it – and died for it. The pages of history are now stained by his blood ... but two generations of black people, and a black American president, have reason to be grateful. They live in the good of what that great man saw. Dreamers often leave their mark on society – not just by what they achieve, but by the terrible price they have to pay to achieve it.

Something happened to me that day. I suddenly realised that if God was the God of the impossible, why shouldn't my dreams come true? Maybe the things I longed for weren't just the product of my vivid imagination. I'd received a wake-up call.

Dr King's rallying cry prompted me to re-evaluate my 'impossible' dreams. I asked God if He had put them there – and if He had, whether He wanted to help me make them become reality. As time went by, I became convinced that God wanted me to see those dreams fulfilled. He can achieve the impossible for me – and for you.

I started to speak about dreams and visions early on in my ministry – and the message has never really changed. That's why I have written this book – to encourage you to revive your broken dreams and to dream new ones. If just half the dreams in Christians' hearts were fulfilled, we could have revolutionised the world for Jesus Christ years ago.

## God's will? Or God's won't?

Most Christians find it difficult to accept that their dreams come from God. If you ask someone, 'What's God's will for your life?' they frown and become intense. They believe God's will can only be achieved with clenched teeth and iron resolve. It's certainly not something to enjoy. They believe enjoyment is of the 'flesh', and can't possibly be God's will. But that's an awful travesty of the truth, probably the result of convoluted thinking and erroneous teaching. The Bible makes it clear God's will is … 'good, perfect and acceptable' (Rom 12:2) – not just to Him, but to you, too. Yet so many believe that God's will is 'good, perfect and unacceptable'!

Grace and I avoid asking people, 'What's God's will for your life?' Instead we ask, 'What's your dream?' They find that easier to answer – and are eager to tell us about places they want to go and the things they want to do. Sadly, though, we find they haven't dared to pursue their dreams, in case they weren't 'God's will'. They see God's will like a tightrope – one false step and all will be lost. So they never make that first step.

We say to people, 'Maybe you're dreaming about the things that God wants you to do.'

'But that seems so fanciful,' they reply.

'That's right,' we tell them. 'God's in the business of being fanciful. He wants to use your imagination.' We don't always give the Holy Spirit time to plant thoughts in our minds and develop them through our imaginations.

Psalm 40:8 looks ahead to the time when Jesus would … 'delight to do the will of his Father' – and that's what He did. Doing God's will delighted Him – and delighted God, too.

In Matthew 7:14, Jesus speaks about a 'narrow way that leads to salvation'. But He wasn't referring to God's will. It's *us* who have made His will a narrow path, when it is often a broad meadow where we can relax, enjoy ourselves and stretch our legs. Few people discover God's will for their lives – they've settled for a warped version of the truth.

People often cried out to Jesus to be healed. And He never asked them, 'Are you sure that's God's will?' Instead, He asked, 'What do you want me to do for you?' That's a question the Lord wants to ask many people about their dreams and desires.

## Dreaming about Jesus

Luke Chapter 2 recounts the day when Mary and Joseph brought their tiny new baby, Jesus, to the Temple to be consecrated to the Lord, in line with the Law and Jewish customs. As they entered the Temple Courts an old man, Simeon, approached them. Like all devout Jewish people, he longed to see the Messiah, the one who would bring peace and establish a rule of righteousness and justice among His people.

Simeon was a dreamer, too. He was in touch with God and he knew he would see this Messiah before he died. He held that dream in his heart – and waited. And decades later, he saw this young couple carrying their baby into the Temple Courts and knew his time had come. Maybe a still, small voice said to him, 'This is the one you have been waiting for!'

He was hardly able to contain his excitement as he hurried towards the young couple. He stopped them, perhaps muttered a few words of introduction and then said these gripping, prophetic words: 'Sovereign Lord, as you have promised, you now dismiss your servant in peace. For my eyes have seen your salvation, which you have prepared in the sight of all people, a light for revelation to the Gentiles and for glory to your people Israel' (Luke 2:29-32). In those few brief moments, Simeon's dream became reality. God had fulfilled His word.

Mary and Joseph must have wondered what the old man meant. But any lingering doubts were removed by what happened next.

There was another 'senior' in the Temple Courts that day. Anna was 84. Her husband had died just seven years after they had married, and since then, she had devoted her life to worshipping God night and day. What a woman! The Bible calls her a prophetess.

Just as Simeon finished speaking, she went over to Mary and Joseph and announced that this baby, Jesus, was the one who would redeem Jerusalem. Her dreams had come true, too!

Imagine the smile on God's face that day. And maybe there's a lesson there, as well, about the importance of giving us seniors a voice in churches. We might have more revelation than you realise!

### The dream for your family

We encourage parents to tell their children about the dreams they have for them. Some are reluctant because they don't want to force their children into a mould. But how can it be wrong for a child to hear God's dreams for them? If parents don't shape their children's dreams, society will do it instead. It will bombard them with messages like, 'Get a good, secure, well-paid job, a good pension, a nice house with all the modern appliances and a little bit of money in the bank for a rainy day'. Or maybe it will feed them with something more sinister … 'Take those drugs … sleep with her … get what you can for yourself …'

If parents leave a void in their children's hearts, the world will fill it! Where are the parents who dream of their sons and daughters being missionaries, evangelists or pastors? I am convinced there are plenty of parents who have aspirations for their children, but they cannot believe God is big-hearted enough to make their hopes become real.

We encourage parents to pray for their children, to tell them what's in their hearts for them, to prophesy to them and to pronounce blessings over them. We also encourage them to pray for their children when they are asleep. It's a moving and intimate moment as a parent stands in the semi-darkness and prays. I wonder how many parents have poured out their hearts to God during those special moments? All parents should take the chance to see their dreams and aspirations worked out for their children.

## Never too young to start

Children should be encouraged to dream for God, too. They are often more in tune with the Holy Spirit than adults. Christian parents should put a world map in their children's bedrooms and encourage them to ask God, 'What part do you want me to play in this world? Where do you want me to go? What do you want me to do?'

The eight-year-old son of a friend of ours did just that. Then he boldly told his dad one day, 'God wants me to go to South America.'

With a wry smile on his face, the dad replied, 'Well, son, South America is a big place. You will have to be more specific.' The boy went away and prayed about it – and returned to his dad with the names of three countries.

It would have been easy for the boy's dad to fob him off. But he didn't. He believed his young son was capable of hearing from God. The boy saved his pocket money, Christmas money and birthday money until he was 13 and then his dad took him to one of our projects in Brazil. The visit helped him to see that he was called to be a resource. He's now a very successful businessman with a big heart to see God's Kingdom established. That's what I call pursuing dreams!

## Dreams within marriages

When we have families together in meetings, we sometimes get the husband and wife to face each other and lay hands on each other – not for a cuddle … there are plenty of other opportunities for that! We ask the wife to prophesy to her husband and voice the things that she longs to see happen in his life. Wives don't find this too difficult.

Then we ask the husbands to do the same for their wives. Sadly, husbands are not always so aware of their wives' dreams. Maybe they are selfishly pursuing their own goals and expecting their wives to trail along behind?

During these times, promises re-surface … things that God told couples when they were first converted, or when they got married. And it's so exciting to see these dreams come alive again. Psalm 37:4-5 says, 'Delight yourself in the Lord and he will give you the desires of your heart. Commit your way to the Lord, trust in him and he will do this.'

### Dreams on tap

No dream is too small for God. Sometimes it's the 'small' things that make a big difference.

We had a dear lady in Chadwell Christian Mission named Olive Peters. When she was a young lady, she had a dream to go to India. And when she was in her 60s, she eventually got there with Ernie, her husband. They helped at an orphanage run by Jochen Tewes.

But Olive cherished another dream. It was not a big dream – just an improbable one!

For most of her Christian life, she had moved in circles where dancing was frowned upon as worldly and sinful. But one day she told me that she had longed to tap-dance, ever since she was a girl. I thought, 'Why not?' and encouraged her to go to tap-dance lessons.

She enrolled on a beginners' course and had to learn alongside people a lot younger than herself. But that didn't put Olive off. She learned to tap-dance – to professional standard! And sometimes, in our meetings Olive would put on her tap shoes and you could hear the tap, tap, tap as she danced before the Lord. She continued tap-dancing to the day she died in her early 80s.

Olive's story shows how God can take seemingly insignificant dreams and make them realities. He's interested in every aspect of our lives and wants us to be completely fulfilled.

We shouldn't limit what God wants to do for us. We can become so 'spiritual' that we miss the simple things He wants us to enjoy. We are made in the image of our Creator – and that means being creative, too! It doesn't matter how ridiculous your dreams might seem. If you share them and speak them out, they may well come true.

## CHAPTER 4

# IN ABRAHAM'S FOOTSTEPS

### Actions have consequences

Abraham was a dreamer. He was also a failure – just like the rest of us.

He is certainly one of the heroes of faith – a man who stands as a giant on the pages of Scripture. When God told him to do something, he did it, even when those commands were mystifying, difficult or appeared downright unreasonable. He pursued his dream and fathered a nation and three religions. Without him, you wouldn't be reading this book, and I wouldn't have written it!

While we may yearn to follow in his footsteps, we can certainly learn from his mistakes. His successes shaped human history for the better. But his mistakes also shaped it for the worse. In the same way, many decisions we make can have consequences, for us and for others.

God clearly told Abraham and his wife, Sarah, they would have their own son, even though it seemed impossible because they were too old. A son was the only way God could fulfil His plan for Abraham's life. But time went by and Sarah did not conceive. The longer they waited, the more desperate Sarah became. Who can blame her?

But her culture also gave her an 'acceptable' way out – a barren woman's husband was allowed to sleep with someone else to produce an heir. And that cultural influence ultimately determined her actions more than God's promise. In Genesis 16:2 she reached the limit of her patience, and in frustration she said to Abraham, 'The Lord has kept me from having children. Go, sleep with my maidservant. Perhaps I can build a family through her.'

Abraham certainly didn't protest too much. He slept with Hagar – and Hagar conceived Ishmael. But the unfortunate child was a bone of contention between Sarah and Hagar even before he was born. He certainly wasn't the joyful fulfilment of Abraham and Sarah's desires – he was nothing but trouble! And historically, Ishmael and his descendants have lived up to God's prediction in verse 12 of the same chapter. 'He will be a wild donkey of a man, his hand will be against everyone, and everyone's hand against him, and he will live in hostility towards all his brothers.'

## Breaking the door down

There's a lesson for us in this story. We're all capable of producing an 'Ishmael' – in fact they're easy, and very pleasant, to conceive! It's easier to produce an 'Ishmael' than to do God's will.

But what's an Ishmael? Well let's be clear – it's never a *person*. God wants to bless people, not label them as a curse! No, an Ishmael is the product of our flesh … something born out of impatience and striving. It's something that is produced by human reasoning rather than by faith.

It might be a project, a church plant, a decision or a career move … something that we believe is God's will to the extent that we'll break the door down to make sure it happens.

We can produce an Ishmael the same way Abraham and Sarah did.

It starts with God's promise. He tells us something and we get excited about it. We walk on air for a few days, our hearts full of faith. We dream of seeing that promise fulfilled – and there's nothing wrong with that.

But then time goes by and the initial excitement wears off. The promise fades. We become frustrated and impatient. God did say it – didn't He? Of course He did. Then why isn't anything happening? Before long we find ourselves trying to give God a hand. We engineer situations and circumstances to bring about His promise. We do His job for Him, and we end up with an Ishmael. It's a product of flesh rather than faith, of lust rather than love and manipulation rather than the miraculous. And once you've created an Ishmael, you're stuck with it.

Hebrews 11:6 quite clearly tells us that without faith, it is impossible to please God. When things aren't happening quite as we imagine they should, we must exercise our faith by patiently trusting God's promises.

## Don't force God's hand

I came frighteningly close to producing an Ishmael. Praise God, I didn't. But I tried to force God's hand with His promises for my life – and if I had succeeded, I don't believe Links would have developed the way it did.

Most dreamers are like Abraham – they love to make things happen. I waited five years for some 'action' after God gave me that first vision of Africa. To me, that was a very long time. I got impatient. But one day, I thought my moment had finally arrived.

I loved watching films from the T.L. Osborn Evangelistic Association. They showed vast crowds at meetings in different countries. Hundreds of people committed their lives to Christ and many were miraculously healed. One film really stirred me. It showed meetings in Ghana. I could almost feel myself on the platform like T.L. Osborn, preaching to thousands of Africans. So imagine how excited I was when an opportunity arose to meet the T.L. Osborn organisation's UK representative. My imagination ran riot. At last the door was opening. I was on my way to Africa!

I met the man and told him about my dreams. He listened, and told me that to start with, I would travel the UK showing films and promoting the association's work. My understanding was that I would eventually go to Africa. My hopes were flying high. Something was happening!

I was right. Something *was* happening. I was forcing the issue.

Fortunately, God stopped me. My enthusiasm turned into a growing sense of unease. I wasn't clear where the finance would come from. I had just got engaged to Grace. How would the work affect our relationship? I had a strong sense that I was pre-empting God. I reconsidered, and dropped my plans.

Yes, God had put a dream about Africa in my heart. But He showed me that I would go when He opened the door. I was not to engineer it.

I was gutted. But looking back, God did me a huge favour.

### The mission on our doorstep

I began to realise I didn't need to go to Africa to preach and see miracles. My mission field was on my doorstep until God said otherwise. I had to learn the difference between pursuing a dream and trying to fulfil it yourself.

Yes, pray about those dreams, walk through doors that God opens, and take the opportunities that He presents. But don't let impatience drive you ahead of Him. An Ishmael will cause you nothing but frustration and heartache – and as Abraham found, once they're born, you can't get rid of them.

We must rest in the fact that if God really has spoken, He will make things happen when He's ready – and more importantly, when He knows that *we're* ready. We should leave things in His hands until then – even though, like me, you may tear your hair out with frustration!

An Ishmael will never produce spiritual fruit. It can't – for things that are conceived in the 'flesh' remain flesh, no matter how much we pray about them. And things of the flesh are in permanent conflict with the things of the Spirit (Gal 4:29). An Ishmael can never be the fulfilment of God's promises. We may end up with an Ishmael AND God's promise … just like Abraham did. Living with both will be as complicated and troublesome for us as it was for him.

## Dogged obedience

Grace and I used to own a dog, and I had varying degrees of success getting it to obey me. Demons were far more submissive to our commands than our dog ever was! I was the typical dog owner. Tim used to take me for a walk, straining at the leash, while I bravely shouted, 'Heel, heel!', with absolutely no response. Then I'd allow Tim off the leash and he'd charge off like a mad thing, disturbing little children playing games and getting involved in fracas with other dogs. I'd shout and bellow, but Tim ignored me. He only obeyed when I placed the leash around his neck, yanked him firmly away and gave him a good scolding.

Then I'd get home and we'd watch a TV programme called *One Man and His Dog*. It was a competition between shepherds, to see who could control their dog the best. They had to herd some sheep round a course, fulfilling certain criteria along the way.

We used to watch the relationship and communication between the shepherds and their dogs with amazement. The shepherds used a certain tone of voice or a special whistle, and the dogs knew exactly what to do. The shepherds' sounds were unintelligible to the untrained ear, but the dogs heard them and understood.

We must learn to obey our Master, the great Shepherd, in the same way. We must be sensitive to His commands and only respond when we hear His 'still small voice'.

If we do that, the job will get done easier and quicker. The alternative is to pull at the leash like Tim, or even charge on ahead and end up in all sorts of trouble. Pursue your dream, but do not run ahead of God!

## Passing the test that matters

Abraham got it wrong with Ishmael. But he certainly got it right with Isaac. He faced his sternest test – and came through strongly.

The tense and heartbreaking story is recounted in Genesis 22. By this time, God had kept His promise – Isaac had been born and was a young man. Things were looking good for the family. But then God spoke these chilling words: "'Take your son, your only son Isaac, whom you love, and go to the region of Moriah. Sacrifice him there as a burnt offering on one of the mountains I will tell you about.'"

God certainly laid it on thick, reminding Abraham that Isaac was his only son, the one he loved. Abraham lived in a culture where children were sacrificed to other gods. Was Yahweh no different? Had he really heard correctly? The Lord had promised Isaac, now He wanted to remove him – horribly and permanently. All of Abraham's dreams were embodied in this one life. Abraham's emotional reaction is not recorded. But Grace and I know what ours would have been – the same as yours, probably.

Abraham got up the next morning and did what God had said. It could not have been easy, though. I doubt if he slept that night. He must have wrestled with his conflicting thoughts and emotions through the lonely hours. But he was prepared to obey. The only way God could keep His promise was to raise Isaac from the dead. Hebrews 11:19 confirms it: 'Abraham reasoned that God could raise the dead, and figuratively speaking, he did receive Isaac back from death.'

So Abraham bound Isaac and laid him on an altar he had prepared. But as he was about to plunge a knife into his son's body, the angel of the Lord stopped him. Yet Abraham was prepared to do it – to lose his son and let his dream die. By this stage in his life, God was more important to him than anything else.

Then the angel of the Lord spoke to Abraham a second time. In verse 16 we read, '"I swear by myself," declares the Lord, "that because you have done this and have not withheld your son, your only son, I will surely bless you and make your descendants as numerous as the stars in the sky and the sand on the sea shore. Your descendants will take possession of the cities of their enemies, and through your offspring all nations on earth will be blessed, because you have obeyed me."'

My prayer is that God gives us the grace to surrender our dreams to Him – completely. If we do, God will do for us what He did for Abraham. He'll restore those dreams – and He'll multiply them.

It's tough love. But death is always followed by resurrection.

### What are your priorities?

This emotional story teaches us one vital thing – the Lord is more important than any dream, no matter how big or significant it might be. We must be willing to let our dreams die if God says so.

Grace and I had to learn that harsh lesson with regard to not having our own family as we explain in Chapter 8. And God has brought many other people to a similar place. What do we desire more? To see our dreams fulfilled, or to obey God? It's easy to say, 'Of course, God's more important.' But can we truly lay down our own desires and trust God?

Grace and I get concerned when we see people fighting to save their project, their plan, their dream. Yes, of course it means a lot to them. But you can see by their attitudes and actions that it doesn't belong to God any more. It's theirs – and they'll kill you if you touch it!

A great friend of mine, John Barr, got it right. If some plan or project went wrong, he'd say, 'If God's in it, it'll be fine. And if He's not – well, who wants it anyway?' That attitude helped him to keep a hold on the precious things that God had given him. It's a quality we can all learn from.

# CHAPTER 5

# BRING ON THE GOOD TIMES – AND THE BAD

### Mum's the word

Mothers have high hopes for their sons. They want them to grow up into men they can be proud of. My mum was no exception. She also had a habit of knowing more about my future than I did!

God told her about two significant things in my life, and both were fulfilled.

When Grace was 24, she went to Bethel Pentecostal Church in Dagenham. But the nearby Elim Church urgently needed Sunday school teachers, so Grace decided to help. She told Bethel's minister she was leaving. He didn't see things Grace's way, but her mind was made up, and off she went.

My mum spotted her the first day she walked into the Elim Church, and decided that she was the right girl for her Norman. How did she know? She hadn't even spoken to the girl! But God had evidently spoken to my mum. She prayed about a possible relationship with a lot of enthusiasm.

Grace got involved with the Good News Team, and when she first met me, she thought I was the most big-headed person she had ever encountered. This Norman Barnes knew everything, always wanted to take charge and was more than secure in who he was. I freely admit she was right!

I also had this habit of kissing the girls hello and goodbye. A holy kiss, of course! But Grace made it plain through friends that if I tried it with her, I'd get a smack round the face! I got the message – and I didn't dare find out if she meant it!

But a romance blossomed and within six months we were engaged. I was only 18 though, so Grace, being a very proper lady, decided we would have to wait until I was 21 before we could marry. That was in 1964 – the year the Beatles were starting out on their road to fame. My mum's first dream about me had been fulfilled.

## A short-lived honeymoon

Our wedding at Dagenham Elim Church was a wonderful day – one of those occasions when you sensed a twinkle in God's eye. But we had to come home early from our honeymoon because we ran out of money. We had one halfpenny between us! And when we arrived back at our rented flat, we didn't have any food, either. We lifted our hearts to God and decided to go and see my mum.

We didn't tell her about our predicament, but out of the blue, she gave us a load of groceries she'd received in an offer at the supermarket. We accepted them gratefully, and that was how our walk of faith began.

We've often had to 'pray in' our food. We learned to trust God in the small things, and gradually had faith for more. Eventually, we were able to impart faith to other people. It was exciting – though scary at times!

We actually sat down to eat dinner off empty plates on two occasions – we didn't have any food to put on them! The first time, we were broke. We had our tithe money in the tin, but we were determined not to spend it. So we prayed … and our landlord knocked on the door.

'Do you fancy a couple of plates of stew?' he asked. 'My wife's cooked too much and we've got some to spare!' Needless to say, we said yes! And it was lovely stew, too.

The other time we could only find vegetables for dinner – and I wasn't ready to become a vegetarian! But an old school friend, Brian Davis, stopped by. 'God told me to buy you some steak,' he announced – and plonked a bag containing two lovely steaks on the table. You never forget things like that.

Once, I drove a motorcycle for three days without any petrol in the tank! We needed to go to the mission three miles away, but we didn't have any money for petrol and the tank was bone dry. There wasn't a drop inside.

I was indoors wondering what to do, when I glanced out of the window and saw Grace in the garden, laying hands on the motorbike and praying over it! I couldn't recall anything quite like that in Scripture (apart from the 'roar of Moses' Triumph'!) … but I had a choice. I could either go out, put my arm round her and say, 'Nice try, love.' Or I could join her in faith.

I chose the faith option. We put on our motorcycle gear, got on the bike, kicked the pedal – and it started! And it kept going, without any fuel, for another three days! Eventually some money arrived in the post, so I drove to the garage – and the 'prayer-fuel' ran out just as I drove up to the pump.

With the price of petrol these days, I sometimes wish Grace would pray like that more often!

## Our dream home?

Most married couples dream of owning their own house. We were no different, and made tentative enquiries about buying somewhere. But I didn't earn enough for a mortgage, so we reluctantly dropped the idea.

We heard there was a flat available a few miles away, but 100 people had already put their names down for it. We added ours to the list. The agents drew up a shortlist of two – and we were one of them. We fully believed that God had given us the flat, but just to be on the safe side, we prayed, 'Lord, if it is not Your will, we don't want it.' We didn't really mean it, though! When we heard that the flat had gone to the other couple, we hit rock bottom.

My mum was disappointed, too. My sister was buying her own house and my mum felt it wasn't fair. In desperation she prayed, 'Lord, Norman and Grace love and serve You, but don't even have a home of their own. It can't be right!' As she waited on God, He gave her a vision of a building with a hall and a stage. The stage had blue curtains, and the hall had brown chairs. There was a two-bedroom flat attached to the building.

The vision was so vivid, she confidently told us, 'Norman, you're going to be a pastor.' I was angry and told her, in no uncertain terms, 'I don't want to be a pastor, I want to be an evangelist.' But she held the dream in her heart and prayed about it.

## The job I didn't want

My good friend, John Noble, was a member of the Good News Team, and he was invited to pastor the Chadwell Christian Mission, in Chadwell Heath, East London. He turned it down, but said Grace and I might be suitable.

I was invited to preach and my mum and dad came along, too. As we walked in the building, my mum said, 'This is the place I saw in the vision.' She asked the secretary if there was a two-bedroom flat attached to the building. There was.

'You will be pastor here one day,' she told me.

'I will not!' I replied angrily. 'I've told you before, I don't want to be a pastor. I've got no time for it, and certainly not here! I don't want to care for all these old people. Anyway they haven't invited me.'

'They will,' my mum replied, with infuriating confidence.

You've guessed it – before long I received a letter inviting me to be their pastor. It was ridiculous! I was only 24 and a dedicated Pentecostal! What possessed them to ask *me* to do the job? I didn't know what to do. Eventually I wrote back saying I would pray about it.

Then I panicked. I only had six sermons, which I used on a rota. As far as I was concerned, six sermons covered everything I wanted to say. I just made sure I never preached at the same place more than six times!

But I figured that if I became pastor of the Mission, I'd have to preach at least twice a week – 100 sermons a year! There couldn't be that many talks in the Bible. It was hard enough getting one sermon together. And anyway, I preferred the 'hit and run' approach.

I was still in turmoil when Grace and I went to a conference where a man called Edgar Trout was speaking. I went out for prayer and he told me, 'The Lord is calling you into something and you are worried about not having the words to speak. If you will wait on God and be faithful, He will give you His word.' I was really encouraged, and believed what he said for all I was worth.

The Mission asked if we could go for a three week trial 'to preach with a view'. I won't tell you my reaction – I really didn't want to go. So I tried to preach myself *out* of the job. I was strong, fiery, and controversial. I gave it to them between the eyes on prevailing prayer, healing, and the baptism in the Spirit … anything to change their minds.

At the end of the three weeks, the congregation had to vote me in or out. There were only 15 of them, but some helpers mysteriously emerged especially for the vote, like they do in the House of Lords. Not to be outdone, I gave God even more conditions. 'To be absolutely sure, I am putting out a fleece. I want a 100 per cent vote in favour of Grace and me taking over. If there is one "no" vote, or an abstention, I won't go.' I was really pushing things to the limit – but the Lord was up for the challenge. The vote was 100 per cent in favour!

Mum was delighted. I was deflated! But eventually we got to the place where we could pray, 'Lord, we're not happy about it, but if this is where You want us, we'll obey.' So my mother's second dream was fulfilled. I started to realise who I took after.

### Grace finds grace

Grace was petrified about being a pastor's wife. But she had to look and act the part, even though she didn't feel comfortable with it. So she studied other ministers' wives, noting how they managed to smile in public, never raised their voices and never lost their cool. This wasn't easy for Grace, for she was down to earth and said what she felt. But she eventually managed to present the right image most of the time!

Once she was invited to a women's 'World Day of Prayer'. It was bitterly cold, with snow on the ground and so she put on boots, a scarf and a winter coat. But all the other women were wearing their finest apparel, leaving Grace feeling very ashamed of her appearance.

While she was there, someone asked her where she was from. She told them. 'Oh, they have a new minister, don't they?' the lady asked.

'Yes, that's right,' said Grace, not giving anything away.

'Could you ask the minister's wife if she would come and speak to this group?'

'Of course!' she promised.

The minister's wife duly accepted the invitation – and returned to speak, dressed in all *her* finery!

## Learning the hard way

I'd taken the job as a pastor – but spent most of my time doing manual work!

The Mission needed rewiring, redecorating and refurbishing. We worked day and night. I gave up my job in Westminster, London, to become a self-employed builder and decorator, so I could give the church more time. I didn't earn much and it was a real step of faith. We just about had enough money for the groceries, and prayed in everything else. We saw God care for us in many wonderful ways.

It would have been easier had we moved into the Mission flat. But it was occupied by other people for a year, so we often walked several miles to get to meetings as we couldn't afford public transport. Then my mum had another word from the Lord. 'You will be in the flat in February,' she prophesied. And we were … though a year later than she expected.

'You got the month right, Mum,' I told her, 'you were just a bit out on the year!'

Still, my mum saw God's wisdom. 'If you'd moved straight into the flat, you'd have made your home your priority,' she told us one day over a cup of tea. 'But if you've got to wait a year, you can give yourselves to the work and make people your priority.'

She was right – again! Most of the folk at the Mission were elderly, and despite my anger and reluctance, Grace and I learned to care for them. We often sat with them through the night as they died, watched them pass away, and then laid them out. In fact, we were so good at it, the local undertaker offered us some work! Although it was traumatic, we learnt a lot about God, the reality of the Gospel in people's lives, and the peace of the Lord.

Caring for people took its toll, though. A member of the Mission became ill and we sat up all night, caring and praying for him. Then in the morning, I went to work. This went on for three days and nights. I didn't sleep at all. One day, while I was working on a roof, I found myself drifting into sleep. It dawned on me that I might be overdoing it. Fortunately, I did not fall off! That would have given a whole new meaning to the expression 'dropping off to sleep'!

When I arrived home, Grace opened the front door and I pitched forward and fell headlong into the hallway. She managed to drag me to bed where I slept for 24 hours. Grace momentarily wondered if I was dead but I woke up, had something to eat and then slept for another 24 hours. I am convinced it was that long sleep that saved me from a breakdown.

However, I still collapsed another three times during the following weeks. Once again I asked myself why I was flogging myself at this Mission, when my call was to Africa and beyond. My patience was sorely tested.

The Mission were concerned about me and offered to pay me a part-time wage. But I collapsed again, so they decided I should work for the church full-time. I received £10 a week, although some members asked if I could live on less!

We still had to pray for all of our food, clothing and other essentials. We only had one carpet, so we carried it from room to room! Guest speakers stayed in the first room that we decorated – with our one carpet proudly displayed on the floor.

One of our first visitors was Cecil Cousens, a prophet who brought a ministry of faith. He became a father figure to us and spoke at our 'ordination'. He knew about our desire to serve God and about my dreams, and on one visit, he prophesied to us.

He told Grace she would no longer be a Martha, but a Mary, who would sit at Jesus' feet. This really spoke to her about her need to be doing things all the time. Then he told me God would change me from a lion to a lamb. This challenged me about the way I dealt with people and helped me tackle my impatient streak. I became more content that God would work things out in His own time. All I had to do was get on with the job in hand.

## The world begins in Goodmayes

Abraham had a dream. He was going to father a great nation. His descendants would outnumber the stars in heaven and the grains of sand on the seashore. He was confident, and in faith he moved his whole family to another land.

But when he got there nothing happened, apart from a famine. Not exactly encouraging!

Maybe Abraham sat in his tent at night, reflecting on God's promises and thinking, 'What on earth am I doing here?' Perhaps he wondered if he'd got it wrong. Here he was, without a child, and he certainly wasn't getting any younger – neither was his wife. In fact Romans 4 tells us his body was 'as good as dead' and Sarah's womb '*was*' dead'. Hardly encouraging signs for a couple who wanted to start a family.

I can identify with any doubts he may have had. God had given me a vision of Africa, and here we were, in glorious Goodmayes, a forgotten area sandwiched between Ilford and Romford. I was the pastor of a Mission that was being phased out by its trustees. We asked the Lord, 'What are we doing here?' many times.

But gradually I began to realise I must prove myself trustworthy in small things – then God would trust me with bigger tasks. Meanwhile there was plenty to do. My mission field was on my doorstep – the same as yours is!

## Good news to the poor

There was a young girl called Christine who was a teacher in the Sunday school. When Grace first saw her, she didn't ask, 'Who's that?' but, 'What's that?' Chris had bleached, blonde hair, had plucked all her eyebrows and wore very heavy make-up. But she regularly attended Sunday services, and gave her life to Christ when I preached about His second coming during the six day war in Israel.

Her fiancé was a young man called John Norton, and he wasn't too impressed by her conversion – he found it hard because she became so different. When they went to the pub with their friends, Chris refused to go in and sat outside in the car. This made John even angrier, and he was really against the Mission. But we were all convinced Chris was doing the right thing by 'making a stand'.

Sometimes, John came to our meetings, but usually stormed out before the end. He could not cope with them. But he began to read the New Testament, and one evening, he came to a meeting where Arthur Campbell was preaching. John responded to an appeal to accept Jesus as Lord of his life.

He and Chris became our very close, firm friends. They were very influential in the life of the Mission and eventually pastored it for a number of years during the late 1980s and 90s.

God started to birth another dream in our hearts. We wanted to see a thriving church … one that would be a living demonstration of Jesus' love and power. We were all very committed. And Sundays certainly weren't a day of rest!

We started the day with a prayer meeting, followed by the morning meeting. Then we had a lunchtime prayer meeting, then Sunday school, and another prayer meeting before an open air witness. And if that wasn't enough, we had an evening meeting followed by an after church rally to round off the day nicely! On top of that, people fasted every Sunday.

We prayed over every chair before the meetings, crying to God to fill them. Our prayers were not answered immediately, though. A good number of chairs were still empty when the meeting began, so I used to remove the last six rows. But when I came out to start the service, people had put them back!

The meetings were not without difficulties. There were arguments about who would sit where. And when I preached, one deaf old man often banged his stick on the floor and said loudly, 'You don't have to shout!' … while others cried out, 'Speak up, we can't hear you!'

But the congregation grew. People brought their friends. We preached on every street corner and delivered leaflets to 6,000 people in the area, not once, but twice! Gradually, folk got saved. The church prayed and fasted over Easter every year. No hot cross buns and Easter eggs for us! And God visited us in remarkable ways, just like He did in the youth group prayer meetings in Elim Church in Dagenham when I was younger. Sometimes the Holy Spirit would sweep into the room and we'd all be prostrated on the floor. A number of men, who are now full-time ministers, still remember those prayer meetings. We saw some wonderful answers to prayer, not just then, but in the future. Prayer was the key to everything we did.

## My prayer mentor

I was really fortunate to have someone who taught me how to pray when I first became a Christian. The lessons I learned laid the foundation for everything Grace and I have done since.

Soon after I joined the Good News Youth Team in Dagenham, the leader asked me casually, 'What are you doing Saturday?'

'Nothing much,' I replied.

'Meet me at the Lighthouse Mission in Canning Town at 10am then,' he said. I didn't know what I was letting myself in for! The man concerned was Bernard Tovell. And when I say he taught me how to pray, I really mean it.

I arrived at the cold, dingy old mission hall in Canning Town – one of the most run-down areas in the country. 'What will we do for lunch?' I asked, pensively.

'You won't need any,' replied Bernard, with a twinkle in his eye. Then he handed me a cushion to kneel on – and we prayed through to 5pm without a break! It was torture. My back ached, my legs ached, and it was freezing cold. The cushion didn't really give much protection from the hard, lino-covered floor and my knees were really sore by the end of the day.

We prayed like that most Saturdays for several years. Sometimes some other men joined us. I would kneel next to Bernard, and to begin with, I just listened. At first, he puzzled me – he used to pray by quoting Scripture, sometimes for hours at a time.

I asked myself, 'Why's he quoting Scripture? After all, God knows it already!' Then I realised – he wasn't teaching God the Scriptures. He was teaching *me*! He knew that if I was going to live a life of faith, I'd need to know the Scriptures – after all, faith comes by *hearing* God's word. I can still remember passages he quoted today – and I have learned to use them as the 'sword of the Spirit' when I pray.

Bernard was an amazing man of God – he soaked himself in prayer and evangelism. He'd retired by the time I met him, and he was one of those men who always looked old … white hair, and the wisdom of God to match. He was very shy and quiet … until he preached and prayed! Then he became a different person – bold and uncompromising. A risky preacher! When he preached on the beach, you could hear him 100 yards away.

Bernard didn't theorise about prayer. He did it! There are plenty of theorists around, but the only way to learn about prayer, or anything else, is to be with someone who practises what they preach.

As the decades have slipped by, I've become more and more grateful to God for placing Bernard in my life when He did. I needed a mentor – just the same as Moses, Elisha and Timothy did. Bernard taught me there are no short cuts when you're waiting on God.

## A church of miracles

We prayed for healing at the Mission – and saw miracles.

We prophesied over three women who were unable to have children, and later, all three of them conceived. We prayed for John

Norton who, like me, suffered from short-sightedness, and the Lord healed his eyes. We prayed for many women with gynaecological problems. They were healed and never had to go into hospital.

One notable healing involved a man called Francis, who wore a steel corset because of spinal problems. He came to the Mission, gave his life to Christ, and was healed at the same time. He took off the steel corset and never wore it again.

We also discovered God was interested in 'preventative medicine'. One day while Grace was praying, He spoke to her about Sue, a young woman in the church who was three months pregnant. Grace was taken aback when the Holy Spirit told her Sue's baby would die. She was very distressed and wasn't sure whether she had heard from God.

'What shall I do about this word?' she asked me.

'I don't think God would tell you a baby is going to die without a good reason,' I ventured. 'What's the point in knowing about it for six months, and then saying, "The Lord told us," when it happens? And we can't possibly say to the parents, "Well, actually, your baby is going to die." God is not that kind of God. He must have told us so we can pray the baby won't die.' It seemed logical to me! So we prayed and fasted a day a week, binding the powers of darkness that were trying to take the child's life.

Eight months into the pregnancy, Sue went into hospital and gave birth to the baby prematurely. Grace and I were on tenterhooks, waiting to hear some news. At last the phone rang. The excited father told me, 'I've got a little girl called Natalie! She's 4lbs and is in intensive care in an incubator.' I tried to seem excited, but it sounded grim. I told Grace and we prayed. 'Lord, what are you doing?' we asked in desperation. 'You haven't taken us this far to mock us.'

Within 24 hours, Natalie began to improve. She came out of intensive care, and started to put on weight. Sue asked the staff why she had been born prematurely.

They told her, 'She had the umbilical cord wrapped around her neck four times. If your pregnancy had gone the full nine months, she would have been so big, the cord would have strangled her and she would have been dead at birth.'

So God had saved Natalie's life by allowing her to be born one month early. The cord slipped off her neck easily and she was healthy. Scientists are still baffled by what triggers childbirth. This case provides a clear answer – God does!

The story doesn't end there. Natalie grew up into a lovely young woman, and made plans to marry a guy named Matthew Cope in Romford in 2006. She phoned us a year before the big day, so we could put the date in our diaries. She wanted us to be the first outside the family to know about the wedding! We were so thrilled.

At the wedding reception, her mum, Sue, told us, 'Today would never have happened had it not been for your prayers.' Grace and I were so choked up that we couldn't speak. Imagine, then, our tears of joy when Natalie called some time later to tell us *she* was pregnant! She gave birth to a lovely baby boy in February 2008. The birth was completely normal.

We are so grateful to God for the many healings He did at the Mission. And many of the prayers that we prayed with the congregation are still being answered, decades later.

### Good times

The Mission went from strength to strength. Links International was growing, too. We also started a very successful primary school called Mountain Ash, which had a huge impact on the pupils, parents and the community.

But ... at the peak of its success, we closed it. Why? We couldn't find enough teachers. We prayed, advertised and did what we could ... but to no avail. Eventually, we set a deadline, but no one applied. So we closed the school, with many tears among the pupils, parents, teachers and the church. No one could understand what God was doing ... especially when a teacher applied for a job *two days* after the deadline passed.

We didn't change our minds, though – we would have lost credibility. And we had to believe that if God had wanted the school to remain open, the application would have arrived before the deadline.

We loved that school, and would have been overjoyed if it had remained open. But looking back, God was teaching us important lessons about when to stop and how to live with unanswered questions.

That's something Grace and I have had to do in many areas of our lives and ministries. Not everything is cut and dried.

There was one situation, though, that drove me to the brink of suicide.

# CHAPTER 6

# THE POWER
# AND THE PAIN

The people who wrote the Bible were blatantly honest. They obviously hadn't heard of 'spin doctors'. They wrote frighteningly frank accounts of people's lives – not just their successes, but their weaknesses, failures and sins, too. Their characters are laid bare for the whole of history to read. In this respect, I'm glad I wasn't around in those days for them to write about me!

Take Paul and Barnabas, for example. Paul was reputed to be a small man, but one of the giants of New Testament history. He was a fiery evangelist, clever, and had incredible revelations from the Holy Spirit. He is someone most of us look to for example and inspiration.

Then there was Barnabas, a man with a caring heart and called the Son of Encouragement – the ideal travelling partner for Paul. They saw many turn to Christ, performed miracles and established churches all over the known world.

But they still nearly came to blows!

Barnabas wanted to take his nephew, John Mark, with them on a mission trip. Paul didn't. They had such a fierce disagreement that they parted company. It could have been avoided, but neither man would back down.

I'm so glad that incidents like this are recorded, because they remind us we all have our weaknesses.

My dreams suffered similar setbacks.

One day while I was still pastoring the Mission, I was travelling with my friend, John Noble, in his car. He mentioned he'd been reading Watchman Nee's book about church life and was excited about the concept of meeting in people's homes. I warmed to the idea – in fact I was very enthusiastic about it. But I didn't realise the implications.

John wanted to act on his vision, and felt he should stop supporting the Mission. He wanted to give himself to the embryonic 'house church movement'. Before long, several of the young people we knew wanted to get involved with him.

I was sad, because I was very close to them – and to John. I got desperately hurt. I am not saying that John was to blame. But I couldn't understand why these young people were going with him, or why he couldn't throw his lot in with the Mission and bring them with him.

Around the same time, the issue of law and grace became a hot potato in church life – too hot for many people to handle! The evangelical world believed house churches were so 'free' they allowed virtually anything to happen. Rumours circulated and accusations were made.

On the other hand, house churches thought a lot of evangelical thinking was legalistic, had nothing to do with the grace of God and was a system of man-made rules and regulations.

Grace and I will freely confess now that both we, and the Mission, were very legalistic. John Noble and the house churches did whatever they liked on a Sunday. We just attended meetings. My hurt turned to anger and I became the arch opponent of the house church movement, ably supported by Grace. I preached against it for several years. John Noble and I fell out, big time – just like Paul and Barnabas.

## Healing the hurts

John and I were out of touch for several years – mainly because of the antagonism on my part. But eventually I began to build bridges. I met him and Maurice Smith once a month and poured out my heartaches and hurts. We cleared up many misunderstandings. It was a slow process, but emotional wounds often take time to heal.

Grace still flatly refused to have anything to do with house churches, though. So I went on my own to their Sunday evening meetings and enjoyed the lively, informal gatherings. Grace's only comment was, 'You're going into error. You'll take me to hell.' But her reaction was more out of fear that I'd get hurt again.

The bond between John Noble and I grew stronger, and our friendship was completely restored when we made a covenant with one another. We promised to work together and walk together, and to stick by one other, whatever happened and whatever the cost. That covenant has lasted to this day.

Slowly the Mission found its way into the house church movement. It took time for Grace's hurts to be healed, but John kept reaching out to her and eventually won her heart.

During this transition, the Mission was in a no-win situation. The evangelicals criticised us because we associated with house churches, and the house churches criticised us because we met in a building. That fledgling movement didn't realise then that its membership would eventually outgrow even the largest front room. And now they've come full circle – many are buying their own buildings!

My reconciliation with John put fresh impetus into my dream of developing an effective church. And my involvement with house churches taught me about caring relationships, the oneness of the body of Christ and body ministry. But there was more trouble ahead.

## Testing the foundations

A new teaching emerged based on Juan Carlos Ortiz's book, *Call to Discipleship*. Issues of authority, submission and discipleship were suddenly high on the Mission's agenda and we began to touch new areas of each other's lives. It hurt.

One morning I received a phone call from a leading figure in the Mission, asking me to meet him at his house. I sensed this was going to be more than a social visit, and asked John Norton to accompany me. When we arrived, there were three men waiting to see us – the Sunday school superintendent, the secretary and the treasurer.

'You've asked me to come here so you can confront me,' was my opening line. I was annoyed I hadn't been told there would be three men present.

'No,' they replied, 'we want to ask questions.'

'That's not true,' I insisted.

They began to make all kinds of accusations. 'The presence of God is not in the meetings,' they asserted. They seemed to ignore the fact that people were being saved and healed.

'Well, that's not all my responsibility,' I replied. 'I cannot just clap my hands and bring about the presence of God that you say is lacking.'

The argument continued, and finally the three men said they wanted to take the matter to the church. I was churned up and had a strong sense of foreboding. Everything we'd worked for over the years seemed under threat. But I agreed, on condition that I'd resign if the vote went against me. If it went against them, however, they should either repent or leave.

The church met and voted in my favour. But I didn't feel victorious – 15 people left, including the three men and a couple of deacons. The rest of us struggled to find some kind of emotional stability. It felt as if we'd had a limb amputated. In some ways, we had.

The Mission was small enough to feel the loss of 15 people very acutely, and we lost around 25 per cent of our income, too. It was a period of pain and grief. We needed time to adjust and collect ourselves.

A church split is never pleasant, but one good thing came out of it. A young man called Norman Cook said, 'If that's the truth of the church, I want to know more.' He was saved as a result.

This traumatic time also made us look carefully at whether we had really produced genuine friendships. We realised our church had been built on faulty foundations. It collapsed under pressure.

However, we were determined to act with honesty and integrity. We didn't allow any gossip, and confronted anyone who tried it. We tackled every problem head on, no matter how painful it was.

We also decided to focus on quality rather than quantity in church life. If people from other local churches visited us more than once, we phoned their pastor. This prevented church-hopping. And those who persisted didn't find it easy to 'get in'. We wanted to make sure their motives were right and that God was involved.

## Dreams ... and despair

Our dream certainly took a severe battering during this time. But you can't have the power without the pain. Sometimes you have to let your dreams die, so God can revive them. Gideon said in Judges 6:13, 'If the Lord is with us, why has all this happened to us?' God didn't answer. But He's involved in the good times and the bad.

Eventually, God's pruning bore fruit and our numbers grew, especially among young people.

Grace and I always dreamed of handing the day-to-day running of the Mission to John and Chris Norton. It took a long time, because God had to deal with my insecurities and pride. And the hand-over wasn't easy. But we didn't regret it, and were thrilled when John, Chris and the other leaders began to take charge. By this time, more doors were opening for me in Ghana and beyond, so we were free to travel without worrying what was happening back home. Or at least, that's what we thought ...

## The time I went to hell

I want to tell you about my own personal hell. It's important you realise that being a 'big name preacher' doesn't make you immune from mistakes, failure and some of the bitterest blows that life – and people – can deal you.

This story is my truth, and my perspective. But that doesn't make it right! Other people have their versions of events and I profoundly respect that. I've always said that there are THREE sides to every story: my side, your side – and God's side.

John and Chris Norton had taken over as the Pastors of Chadwell Christian Mission, by then renamed, Oasis Church. But by 1993-4, it was felt that John had taken the church as far as he could. So the leaders asked me to take it into the 'next stage' of God's purposes. They felt I had the vision needed at the time.

I agreed – but didn't think I needed to give up my work with Links International, which involved a lot of travel. And because I was away a lot, I set up report-back structures for other leaders, so I knew what was going on.

Around the same time, the Toronto blessing swept many parts of the world – including Chadwell Heath. I've never known such an amazing outpouring of God's power. On one occasion, a wind swept through the hall, knocked us down – and continued straight through some double doors! It was an astonishing period during which many people's lives were challenged and changed.

I remember praying at the time, 'Lord, I want to see Your glory – whatever it takes.' I didn't realise what it *would* take. The cost was more than I could have imagined.

During this time, I preached a lot about the earthquake, wind and fire, based on Elijah's encounter with God in 1 Kings 19. I told people, 'If you don't bend with the wind of the Spirit, the earthquake will shake you, the wind will break you and the fire will refine you.' I didn't realise the process would start with me. I had to live it, and discover the still small voice of God's glory that only comes when you've yielded and have absolutely nothing left.

## The lowest point

During 1995-96, some of the men in the Oasis told me they didn't like my style of leadership and were going to leave. But I was desperate to avoid a church split, so I said, 'No – you stay. I'll stand down and give you the church.'

I think my offer surprised them, but they accepted it. So I stood down … only not just from my position. I went down … straight into the pit, into a place I never even knew existed, into a place of torment so terrible I can't put it into words.

For the next two years, Grace and I sat in the back row of that church without a role. We weren't asked to preach, to help, or to pray for people. As father and mother of the church, it nearly destroyed us. We felt humiliated, rejected and betrayed.

I went into a pit of depression. I cried myself to sleep, night after night. All my dreams were in ruins. I planned to go into London and throw myself under a train. And it wasn't a cry for help. I meant it.

By 1998, John Noble said it would be best if Grace and I left the Mission – he could see that it was too painful for us to carry on. 'You're too big for this church,' he told us. So we had to go through the agony of saying goodbye to the church to which we'd devoted our lives for more than 30 years.

We had a few minutes to speak, hugged and kissed a handful of close friends … and walked out, amid an atmosphere charged with tension.

I closed the Mission door behind us, looked at Grace, and said, 'It's over.' We went home and sobbed our hearts out. We were absolutely broken. Only two families popped in to see us later that day to see if we were all right. We weren't. We were destroyed and felt lonely and abandoned. Suicide was top of my agenda.

But when you hit the very bottom, God has His man there. Jethro rescued Moses. Barnabas rescued Paul. And a guy called Ken Tune rescued us.

Ken was an old friend – the leader of Dronfield Christian Fellowship in Derbyshire. We phoned him to tell him what had happened, and he came straight down to see us. He walked into our shattered, broken world, and brought God's word.

'All that's been in my mind as I travelled down,' he said, as he sat down in our living room, 'is the earthquake, wind and fire in the book of Elijah.'

His words hit me like a thunderbolt. God had spoken … in a still, small voice.

Suddenly we realised we'd been through the shaking, the breaking and the refining I had preached about. It was like someone switching a light on. It all made sense. It didn't make things any less painful or tragic. But it did help us to see that God was behind the events that had smashed our world and ripped our hearts to shreds.

Ken's word unlocked the situation. Like Jacob, I had wrestled with God. I had sought His glory … and now, I would walk with a limp. The vulnerability of being suicidal changes you … you're never the same again. You never forget that you're dust and that your life really is in God's hands.

God's love can be a terrible love. You don't hear that preached very often these days. But God doesn't change. Taking up your cross means one thing – the death of the things you hold most dear.

Isaac was Abraham's child, the one he loved … the embodiment of his dreams. And yet God told Abraham to lay him on the altar and kill him. Oasis was our special child, the one we loved … the embodiment of our dreams. And we had to let it die in our hearts. The rest was God's responsibility.

## A season of healing

Ken Tune's words didn't act as a magic wand. Our situation was still the same. We had to bear the pain of watching our beloved church from afar. We felt like parents, seeing their children from a distance, not being able to go and hug them and make sure they're OK. I still had to go to Oasis every day – the Links office shared the building. That was tough, too.

Mercifully, we coped financially – the Oasis leaders kindly said they would continue to support Grace and me for the rest of our lives, and we deeply appreciated that. Links also continued to support me – though the catch was that I was the only fund-raiser! So if I didn't raise the funds, I didn't get the support!

Sadly, though, the Oasis leaders did end the financial support to both us and Links. That was another painful time. Grace and I looked back on the occasions we'd gone without to support people in the church, and felt let down. We weren't bitter – just very hurt. But God is the paymaster, and he brought fresh financial support from all kinds of sources. One of them was most unexpected.

The internationally renowned Bible teacher, Joyce Meyer, had somehow heard about Links and offered to support us financially. We were stunned. She gave $12,000 a year to Links and $6,000 a year to Grace and me, for the next five years. We owe her, and the other people who helped us, a debt of gratitude that we'll never repay.

After a while, God moved us on. Two of the guys on the Links board attended Molesey Christian Fellowship in Surrey, and suggested we went there. We weren't that keen – we were too hurt to have much enthusiasm about going anywhere. But we went anyway, and spent some very precious years there. They loved us, cared for us and helped us heal. What wonderful people they were!

Grace and I never thought we'd get over what had happened to us – and in some ways we never will. But the good people at Molesey brought a healing and restoration we never believed possible.

It was hard though, to see Oasis dwindle from 150 to around 25. That broke our hearts. But God works all things together for good for everybody – and I am convinced the last chapter of that story hasn't been written yet.

After six years at Molesey, God directed us to Rustington in Sussex – we needed to plan for our 'retirement'. He blessed us with a wonderful flat on the sea front. We have a balcony overlooking the sea, and spend many happy hours gazing at the waves, the families on the beach, the surfers and the yachts with their brightly coloured sails. Our view is different, every day of the year … what an awesome God He is. And that balcony … it's perfect to use as a pulpit to preach to the people on the beach. One day …

Grace wanted to commute to Molesey, but after praying about it, we felt we should become part of Arun Community Church, based nearby. The Pastor, David Thatcher, made us very welcome and we are so blessed there.

Leaving Molesey was sad … but it also brought healing. The congregation devoted almost our entire last Sunday meeting to Grace and me, and gave us a gift of £500. They presented Grace with some beautiful roses, and sent us out with prayer and prophecy.

### Lessons learned

Amid all the agony and confusion of those years, we had to come to a place where God was the God of the things we did understand – and the things we *didn't* understand.

Life with God wasn't cut and dried for the men and women in the Bible – and it won't be for us. We can expect disappointments, broken dreams, failures and issues that can't be explained. And that doesn't always mean you are out of God's will or have done something wrong.

Circumstances, sin and bad decisions may delay us on our journey, and may even send us down the wrong road. But God promises we will arrive at the right destination. The children of Israel arrived in the Promised Land – even though their route was certainly not God's best.

We can all rejoice in our destination – but we may well have many unanswered questions about the journey. Remember, God is not duty-bound to give us answers. But He *does* give us promises. And they're what matters. Especially when you are going through your own personal hell.

# CHAPTER 7

# FORMING LINKS

## Small steps – big results

I could never have guessed where that first trip to Ghana would lead.

Following God usually means taking small steps and making ordinary decisions that turn out to have massive significance, both now and eternally. God takes ordinary things, and makes them extraordinary. But if you reverse roles with God, and try to do the extraordinary yourself, you run into problems.

Jesus had an ordinary conversation with a woman at a well. But it led to revival in Samaria.

A disheartened fisherman called Peter performed the thoroughly ordinary task of casting his fishing net out of his boat. But his catch was so big, it tore the nets, nearly sank the boat – and produced a revelation.

A man named Ananias made an ordinary house call to a man he'd never met – and Paul had an encounter with the Holy Spirit that changed world history.

My first visit to Ghana was as ordinary as it gets – one ordinary bloke from Dagenham nervously clambering up the steps of a plane. But that trip birthed Links International, which grew into something beyond anything Grace and I could have imagined – the kind of multiplication that only God can produce. Tens of thousands of people have been blessed, saved and provided for in the decades that followed. There's nothing ordinary about that!

We never had a business plan, or any other kind of plan for that matter. But God did! We just took some ordinary steps … and since then, Links has:

- Given away around £1.6million

- Opened offices in the UK, America, Canada, South Africa, and soon in Hong Kong

- Worked in every continent on earth

- Seen many thousands of people saved

These 'guesstimates' don't begin tell the whole story. They're just the things we can calculate and record. You cannot quantify the ripple effect. Links has touched and blessed hundreds of thousands of people worldwide.

I'd love an expert to assess how we did it. He would soon conclude it was impossible for so few people to accomplish so much with so little. Our influence has always been greater than our manpower. But that's how God works. He takes what we've got – even if it is just some bread and a few fish – and multiplies it. He uses mathematical formulae that the world's cleverest brains could never begin to fathom. And all He needs is an ordinary bloke like me, an ordinary lady like Grace, or an ordinary reader like you, to have dreams, pray hard, take steps – and let our extraordinary God do the rest.

## One thing leads to another

I'd have been happy to call it a day after that first trip to Ghana. I'd had the vision, been there, done it, and got the sweaty T-shirt! But that trip made a profound impression on me. I'd experienced Third World poverty first hand – and it wasn't something I could forget. Something deeper was burning in my heart.

Of course, I'd read that two-thirds of the world's people desperately lacked basic sanitation, medical care, education, transport and the most rudimentary forms of technology. But when you see the faces behind those statistics – the children without food, the mothers without hope and the fathers without work – you see things differently. That first journey couldn't be the last one. I had seen the needs, and I couldn't 'unsee' them. How could Grace and I go back to 'normal'?

We soon realised my return from Ghana was just the beginning of the journey.

We'd always been interested in world mission. We invited missionaries on furlough to speak at the Mission and supported and cared for them. But ordinary events shaped our destiny.

## Plenty of ways to care

In Ghana, I was unprepared for the Mills family's ecstatic reaction when I gave them 'trivial' things like tea, coffee, sugar, sweets, soap and toothpaste. They were priceless to this devoted missionary family.

As we got to know David, we discovered that many missionaries didn't get much support from the West. His family lacked simple items like paper, pens, dried milk and basic food. We privately made a note every time they said they needed something, and the list grew longer as we spent more time with them. When I got home, we arranged for the items to be shipped to them.

Once I noticed something was wrong with David's car. He told me it took at least six months to get spares in Ghana. I was determined to help. So when I got back to England, I got the spare parts David needed, and they were in his hands in six weeks. That's one good thing about coming from Dagenham. There are car spares shops everywhere!

We also sent food parcels containing items that were virtually unobtainable in Ghana. And the warm letters of thanks made me realise there was something we could do to help and care for people overseas.

## Spreading the word

We began sharing our experiences with other churches, and people were astonished at the conditions we described – and at what God was doing. It was easy to lose sight of the fact that there was phenomenal growth and great displays of God's power across Africa. It seemed ironic that Christians in affluent countries had so many resources, but were unable to make the same impact with the Gospel as those living in poverty in Africa.

Churches in the UK started giving us money for our friends in Ghana and eventually we needed a separate agency to deal with it. Peter Martin, my close friend, administrator and right hand man, had a flash of inspiration. He suggested we start a work called Links International, since it conveyed our vision. He's come up with several other slogans since – he could have made a fortune in an advertising agency! 'Serving the Church around the world' and 'Together, we can make a difference' were his, too!

So Links was born, not with a fanfare, but with ordinary people having a cup of tea and biscuits in the flat above a mission hall in Chadwell Heath. We wanted to bless people and were often amazed how little things brought such tremendous blessings.

Our contact with Ghana grew stronger. Grace and I went back almost every year from 1981 onwards, and took others with us. Every time we went, we discovered what local Christians and communities needed, and did what we could to help. It just grew and grew!

We found many ways to offer assistance. A Church of Pentecost school in a town called Koforidua had 600 pupils, but very little in the way of teaching materials. Their learning resources made the so-called 'lack' in British schools look like a positive abundance. There was one book per subject for every class, and the children's reading books were kept in the headmistress' room. They were hopelessly out of date and extremely worn.

We returned to England and raised enough money to send reading aids, pens, pencils, rulers – everything, in fact, the children needed. They were delighted.

We could have kept sending more teaching materials, but we learned the importance of asking local church leaders about priorities. The country's needs were so great, we didn't know where to start – but they did. So over the next few years, we sent out everything from generators to printing presses and from clothes to a coach. And we dispatched barrel loads of medical equipment, motor vehicle spares, and two tons of food during a famine.

## Teaming up

We also sent out people, including a newly qualified doctor and his family to work in a medical centre, and another family to set up a vehicle repair workshop and train mechanics to do repairs. This saved the Church of Pentecost thousands of pounds.

But the giving wasn't just one way. We were often embarrassed by the generosity people showed us. Most people lived in dire poverty, yet fed us until we were full. They loaded up our vehicle with fruit and vegetables, and then gave us presents and money. We were overwhelmed, but knew if we refused, they would feel they had not given enough and try to find more. And these were people who did not know where the next day's food was coming from. We knew we could never out-give or out-serve our Ghanaian brothers and sisters. We learned so much from them and I hope we never believe that *we've* got the goods to give to *them*. Every time we go there, we learn from their zeal for evangelism, their faithfulness in prayer, their abandonment in worship and their sheer enthusiasm and exuberance about the things of God.

Links also helped to raise money to bring people from Ghana to the UK. A number of leading pastors visited us, and their stories were a real inspiration and encouragement.

Over the years, God continued to lead us into new challenges, new opportunities and new countries. As a result, six main areas of work evolved.

## 1. Keeping people healthy

We started sending teams of medical specialists into rural areas of Africa and Asia quite early on. To this day, teams of 12 people, comprising doctors, nurses, dentists and opticians, go and spend two weeks in a village somewhere. They train teams in basic healthcare principles, who then go out and train others. The teams really muck in – they stay in the village huts, eat the local food, and experience the delights of the local toilets! However, during their middle weekend we put them in a nice hotel so they can have a shower and a rest before going back into the fray for another week.

The results have been significant. Mortality for children under ten has been drastically reduced in many areas. Regional governments have been keen to work with us, and Nelson Mandela personally invited us to send a team to train 250 delegates in his own village. During the ten years we have been involved in primary healthcare, thousands of people have been trained, and more than 4,000 people have come to faith in Christ.

Let's give you an example that will excite you. Once we took a team into a remote African village called Kasubi in Uganda. The team realised there was a lack of basic hygiene, so they spent the rest of their first week teaching simple principles like washing your hands before you eat.

The team also noticed the latrines were in a dreadful state, and figured there was no point in teaching basic hygiene without doing something practical to help. So we offered to provide $1,000 for new toilets if the village people would build them. Before long, the village had new toilets – complete with basins.

During the visit, the team asked the villagers how many babies had died in the previous year because of bad hygiene. They said there were too many to count.

When they went back 12 months later, they found that just 35 babies had died. And six months later, that figure was down to *zero*! The toilets, basins and teaching on personal hygiene had worked. Stories like this make me want to jump for joy.

This success has been repeated many times in other places. Our emphasis is on *doing* as well as *teaching*. And we don't just leave the Ugandan people to get on with it – there are follow-up visits, so new habits are worked into the fabric of community life.

It's humbling to think we were able to save children's lives. The impact that some of those surviving babies have since made for God and His Kingdom is impossible to quantify.

## 2. Starting small businesses

A small sum of money can make an astonishing difference to a family in poorer parts of the world. The price of your weekly supermarket shop could literally transform the lives of an African family – for good.

Some years ago, we set up a project to help people start small businesses. We give them a loan of between £30-50, which they invest in a project that generates enough money to take a family out of poverty. As a result, children are fed and clothed, daily needs are met, savings accounts are opened and churches receive tithes from the profits.

Eventually, the original loan is paid back and is reinvested in someone else. I guess that's what you'd call recycling money! Maybe some of the big banks that have suffered during the credit crunch should try it – God's economic policies never fail.

These loans help to restore people's dignity and self-respect and empower them to change their lives. So far, we have established more than 3,000 businesses in Uganda, with others in Burundi, Kenya, India, and the Philippines. Two new initiatives have been started in Peru, four in India and other new projects have been launched in Tanzania and Kenya.

Let me tell you the story of a girl called Sarah, a young Ugandan woman. She was a young mother, living in terrible poverty and unable to feed her children. We provided her with a loan and she started up a business selling charcoal. She bought it cheaply and took it back to the city to sell from the roadside.

After a while, though, other people caught on to the idea. But Sarah was smart. She applied for a second loan and set up a wholesale business – and sold charcoal to her rivals! She eventually became self-sufficient and was able to feed and clothe her children, and was also able to buy a plot of land to build her own house. I sense the smile on God's face when He sees outcomes like that, don't you?

### 3. Supporting missionaries

As we met missionaries around the world, we realised they quickly lost contact with the Christian scene back home. And when they returned on furlough, they were often out of touch with current teaching, ministry and songs. Some had a real struggle settling back in.

We also realised many were suffering from real spiritual starvation – they had to find God on their own, and give out constantly, often in the most difficult and testing circumstances.

Once, we visited a dear missionary lady in the Amazon. We had a small battery tape recorder and a Christian music tape with us, so we put it on and spent a wonderful time worshipping the Lord … church, jungle-style.

This gave me an idea. When we got back home, we started sending regular teaching and worship tapes to missionaries overseas. This ministry grew – and now 210 missionaries in 59 countries receive a quarterly package that includes a Christian book, too. These resources are a lifeline in parts of the world where being able to afford a book puts you among the top ten per cent of a nation's wealthiest people.

We often get letters telling us that the package was 'the right thing at the right time'. Parents sometimes have to wait to listen to the worship tape because their children got to it first! Some folk have told us they were about to give up, but the tape encouraged them to persevere.

A group of pastors in a remote part of Africa were asked to do some teaching on HIV and AIDS. The problem was they didn't really know anything about it, so they set aside five days for a prayer retreat to call on God to help them.

At the end of the retreat one of the pastors went home and found that our latest package had arrived. It included the re-printed version of Dr Patrick Dixon's book, *The Truth About Aids*, which contained all the latest global thinking on AIDS from a Christian perspective. It was exactly the material they needed. All those pastors praised God that night, I can tell you.

### 4. Creative ways of raising money

This is a posh name for 'bright ideas'! And some of them really have been bright – straight from the mind of God.

This area of Links' ministry is a mixed bag. We give one-off loans to a variety of schemes. But the rules are they have to sustain themselves or generate income. This means people become self-sufficient – they don't depend on the West for their support.

Neither Grace nor I want to criticise past mission work, but we have sometimes wondered if some of it was colonialism in disguise. People were not taught to become self-sufficient.

Links wouldn't get involved in a scheme to build a hospital, worthy as that might seem. Why? Well, who will provide the money to pay wages and buy medicine and equipment? Who will train the staff to work there? Who will run it and maintain it? Many hospitals and clinics in Africa stand disused because there isn't any money to sustain them. They were built with gifts and good intentions – but these weren't enough.

A pastor once asked us to provide a vehicle because he had to care for a number of churches over a wide area. He was too poor to buy one. But we refused. 'We don't want to make you poorer,' we told him.

He didn't understand. We explained, 'You're telling us you're poor. So if we buy you a vehicle, you'll have to find money for running costs, petrol and repairs. You'll be even poorer than you are now.'

We suggested he trained regional leaders, so he didn't have to care for all the churches himself. But he wasn't very keen on that idea!

We've probably pioneered some new thinking in mission work. We believe our approach is part of reflecting God's unconditional love to the poor.

Once we sent money to start up an Internet cafe in Manila in the Philippines, which is now providing work and training for individuals who live on 'Smoky Mountain', the world's biggest refuse tip. The project also generates income for the organisation working with them.

We've seen some great results in Thailand. We started lychee farms and fish farms in the north, and paid for 600 orange trees in another area. These provide food and a source of income for refugees from Burma – a completely unreached people group.

In southern India, Links provided fishing nets for fishermen recovering from the devastation of the Tsunami and raised £50,000 to rebuild residential accommodation for girls in Chennai.

In Kenya, Links bought a cow for £220. It provided enough milk for an entire school on a rota basis. The clever bit was that the £220 included the cost of having the cow artificially inseminated – so we ended up with two for the price of one, or 'buy one, get one free', as the modern marketing men call it!

It's a real blessing to see how these creative projects change people's lives and communities. We try to use what God's given us wisely, as Jesus instructed in the parable of the talents.

## 5. Working with churches

Links has always been based on relationships, and I believe this has been the reason for its success.

Most importantly, there's the relationship our workers have with God. But there's also their relationships with one another. We never get involved in anything unless it comes from a relationship with someone.

We're not another missionary society. We're into *links*, not impersonal contact. We never help someone to go to another country unless their local church pays their salary, sends them out and prays for them. At times, we provide fares, expenses, expertise and other capital expenditure. Our vision is to extend God's Kingdom through the Church. That's important to us. We want to work together as a body – we bless people, and they bless us. God loves relationships – the first 'Links' he established were between the Father, Son and Holy Spirit, all working in harmony together. Plainly, God has always been into links. We're so privileged He's also into Links!

This approach also creates a clear line of accountability for every penny we're given. Nothing's wasted.

Over the years, we have befriended many churches, but only to help them. There are no strings attached. We believe in partnership without ownership. We train leaders, offer expertise and resources and encourage people on the front line. But we never try to take over. We may provide a one-off blessing, or some kind of apostolic input, and just about everything in between.

Our ethos is not 'How can you help Links?' but 'How can Links help you?'. We're 'mission brokers' – we link people, fix things, and make things happen … just like ordinary blokes from Dagenham do all the time!

## 6. Providing expertise

Links has developed considerable knowledge and expertise, and we are privileged to offer this to other churches.

We now operate a charitable umbrella for 63 churches, individuals, missionaries, organisations and business people in the UK and beyond. This enables them to fulfil their vision and get on with the job, while we take care of the accounts, handle Gift Aid and transfer money abroad for them. We also run training programmes, provide services and offer advice.

Many other projects have sprung up over the years. These merit a book of their own … that comes later!

We sent teams of young people aged 18-plus to countries across the world, to take part in summer projects. They helped in orphanages, worked with children, painted and decorated, and helped with irrigation schemes. Hundreds of young people, some in their gap year, had their first taste of mission work this way. It left a lasting impression on many of them.

Our American friends sent out a team to help build a secondary school in Jamaica. It became so successful the Government used it as a model for other schools right across the country. And they send teachers across the globe to train other teachers. In some countries, they've helped set up the national curriculum.

## Minding their own business?

I'm a great believer in harnessing the skills of business people – and they have been a huge help over the years.

We take them on a five or six day trip to somewhere like India, the Philippines or Africa. It's not a 'cheque book' trip – we're not after their money. We use their expertise to evaluate projects and suggest changes. I tell them to have a nose around. Business people have a 'knower' – they instinctively know if a project will work. They often save us a lot of heartache and wasted money. They ask questions like – is a project feasible? Is the costing right? Is there a market for the produce? Is this the right man for the job?

These trips also help some of these guys learn different values. We took a businessman to a children's home in India where 15 girls lived in a 14ft room with bare floors. Each girl had her own floor mat to sleep on, and a small cupboard for her meagre possessions – and that was it. The man gazed around the room and said to me, 'My son's bedroom is bigger than this – and is crammed full of stuff.' Experiences like this change people's perspectives, just like they changed mine.

Businessmen are impacted by how little it costs to make a massive difference to people's lives. In Uganda, £50 a year can put two families into business. £30 can provide a family with clean water for a year. Many business people spend this on a meal or a round of drinks – it's petty cash to them. But in poor countries, a little can do a lot. That's the joy of supporting Links – anybody can make a difference to someone, somewhere. Even small donations can have a significant impact. God can do all kinds of things with a widow's mite, or the loose change in your pocket.

## How ordinary are you?

Grace and I still find it hard to believe how God took a small operation like Links and used it in such diverse and significant ways. To begin with, we just saw it as an incredible adventure. But we now realise it was a doorway to something far greater. Grace and I have eaten bush rats and snails, been terrified by spiders and have used toilets that would make your hair stand on end – the people on the reality TV show, *I'm a Celebrity, Get Me Out of Here* have it easy, I can tell you! We've been up the Amazon, in the jungle, had dinner with a tribal Prince and stood on the Great Wall of China. During the first half of 2008, Links' cash output was nearly £1million.

And we're just an ordinary couple from Dagenham!

Earlier in this book, I mentioned how God used Joseph. But Joseph was anything but ordinary to begin with. He thought he was a somebody. He boasted. He had an extraordinary coat, dreamed extraordinary dreams, had extraordinary ideas, and made sure everyone knew about them. It took a lot of pain and suffering to make him ordinary enough for God to use him to touch his own family, his nation, and other nations of the world.

I can relate to Joseph. When I started out, I wasn't that ordinary, either. I thought I was a somebody, too. I had loads of confidence. I was always the leader, even at school in Dagenham, where the former England manager, Terry Venables, was in my class! He took his orders from *me*! God had to take me through many trials and tears so I was ordinary enough to use. And He hasn't finished yet. Every time I'm tempted to think I'm extraordinary, God has a way of reminding me that I'm not!

God can use you, too, with the dream He's put in your heart. But are you ordinary enough to allow Him to do the extraordinary with you? If you are, your dreams can shake the world and impact heaven.

When Grace and I started out, our dream was to inspire people to give, to pray and to go – and it still is. Thirty years later, we are still finding new situations, new challenges and new opportunities. Links is a fulfilment of the vision God placed in our hearts. All we can do is humbly acknowledge, 'God has done this, and it is marvellous in our eyes.'

He's been extraordinary.

# CHAPTER 8

# MORE THAN ONE WAY TO HAVE CHILDREN

### The words that broke our hearts

'It's very unlikely that you will ever have children.'

Those stark words hit us like the shock waves from an exploding bomb. Grace had become pregnant, but lost the baby. A specialist from the London Hospital came to our flat to examine her. And this was his bleak prognosis.

Those who are unable to have children will understand our pain. We were dazed. Stunned. Numb. This was not helped by a thoughtless individual who told us it was God's judgement for leaving a certain church.

After the consultant left, we fell into each other's arms and wept. Over the next few days, we tried to console one another. It was an empty, hopeless time.

The Bible records the bitter stories of women who were rather starkly described as barren. We see Rachel, who was desperate to bear Jacob's children and who was jealous of her sister who had four sons. In desperation, she cried out to her husband, 'Give me children or I'll die!' That cry from her heart contained such pain, frustration and torment, and we can understand exactly how she felt.

Then in 1 Samuel 1, we read about a man called Elkanah, who had two wives. One of them, Peninnah, had children. But the other, Hannah, wasn't able to conceive. Peninnah provoked Hannah about it, year after year, until Hannah eventually cracked. She was reduced to tears and would not eat. She endured such agony that 1 Samuel 10:11 tell us, 'In bitterness of soul Hannah wept much and prayed to the Lord. And she made a vow, saying "Oh Lord Almighty, if you will only look upon your servant's misery and remember me, and not forget your servant but give her a son, then I will give him to the Lord for all the days of his life …"'

The Lord was gracious and answered Hannah's prayer. She gave birth to Samuel. But not everyone experiences a miracle like that.

## Too painful to bear

The struggle to conceive children still goes on today. We read in the newspapers about the measures people take when they discover that conventional methods of conception don't work. In desperation, they turn to fertility drugs, test tube babies and even surrogacy – and who can blame them? Their pain is too much to bear.

We knew why we lost our baby. Grace had a history of fibroids. She needed an operation when she was two and another when she was 24. But the problem returned and the fibroids killed our baby. Knowing the reason didn't make the loss any easier.

At her lowest point, Grace recalled an encounter with God many years earlier. God asked her, 'Are you prepared to give up everything for me?'

Grace had pondered before answering. 'Yes Lord, I will give up everything for You – apart from having a family. You wouldn't expect me to do that, would You? After all, that's what You created us for, isn't it?'

That conversation occurred when Grace was around 13. Her parents were Anglicans, and regular churchgoers, but her mother objected to what she considered Grace's 'religious mania', and only allowed her to attend church once a week. Grace had to walk around the local park if she wanted to pray or read her Bible, which she frequently did.

But it didn't really help us to recall that conversation. Our dream of having children still lay shattered. We cried from our hearts, 'Why us?' We couldn't understand what childlessness would achieve. Why was God asking this of us?

Our disappointment turned to anger. 'What kind of God are You?' we cried in frustration. 'We've given up everything for Your sake and now You are asking this of us.'

Eventually, we found peace. We said yes to God's will – but it cost us a great deal and still does, today, 40 years later. However, we added this proviso: 'Lord, if You are really asking this of us, we ask for Your grace to accept it. And we also ask for a spiritual family – sons and daughters in the Kingdom of God.'

God heard that prayer and answered it in ways that were beyond our wildest dreams.

## Hope disappears

By 1978, our lingering hopes of having children disappeared. Grace was taken into hospital for a hysterectomy. But there were complications. Her bowel collapsed because she'd already had so many operations and her condition became critical. A surgeon was rushed through London with a police escort to carry out emergency surgery.

Grace was at death's door. At home, folk prayed, while in the hospital two surgeons operated on her. One worked on the collapsed bowel and the other performed the hysterectomy. It was a miracle she survived.

But Grace has always been a fighter. She resolved to be up and walking round the ward by the next day. And by 12 noon she'd done it. She was equally determined not to let the operation demoralise her. So she went round the other wards, speaking to other patients and praying with them.

A teenage girl in the bed opposite was boasting she'd had two abortions, and her words pierced Grace's heart like a knife. Her initial reaction was not very 'Christian'! But then she realised this young girl needed love. She couldn't allow bitterness to take root in her heart. So she went across to her bed and put her arms around her. The girl wept. The boasting was just a cover for her true feelings. Even in those darkest moments, God's light shone and dispelled some black and ominous clouds.

## New kinds of parents

God used the young people at the Mission to answer our cry for spiritual sons and daughters. We always enjoyed being with them, but submitting to God's will created a break-through in our relationship with them. We became like a mum and dad to many of them. But this was not the complete answer to our prayer.

The turning point came when our good friends, John and Chris Norton, had a baby girl called Victoria. They involved us in almost every aspect of Victoria's life. We often stayed overnight so we could enjoy being with her. In the mornings, Chris fed her and then left us alone to bath her, cuddle her and play with her. And when she was weaned, John and Chris put a cot in our home, so she could stay overnight with us. They let us take Victoria to nursery and buy things with her. Their selflessness filled huge gaps in our hearts and lives.

But it wasn't easy. We had to make ourselves vulnerable and expose the tender areas of our hearts … places that many people without children avoid because it is too painful. Pushing someone else's child down the road in a pram could have been traumatic. But we learned to face our insecurity and pain, find God in our weakness and receive His healing and His grace.

Vicky is now married to James and they have three children of their own. They are the Pastors of Oasis Church, the very same Chadwell Christian Mission that Grace and I pastored all those years ago. We feel so privileged we were able to sow some seeds into her life which are now bearing fruit. She still remembers coming to our flat for those 'special weekends'. They were special for us, too.

Vicky wasn't the only baby we cared for. Grace looked after a twin for a while because the mother couldn't cope with both of her new offspring. To me, this really is church in action – and there are no losers.

### New kinds of families

Looking back, we realise we were actually living the Biblical concept of a 'family'. In our culture, a family equals mum, dad, 2.5 children and seeing some relatives now and again.

But Scripture only talks about 'households' – extended families were the norm. And they included children, relatives, friends, servants, grandchildren and animals, all living together! We'd love to see church families break out of the Western concept of family and live in 'households' – they provide such blessing and support.

One of the reasons Social Services have to care for the young, the elderly and the vulnerable is because families aren't prepared to take them in. Grace and I always encourage parents not to be afraid to let their children go to other people for help, advice and friendship as they grow up. Parents can never provide all the answers to a child's needs. We remember saying things to Vicky that her dad, John, could never have said. If he'd said them, she would have rejected them outright. But if we said them, she thought it was wonderful!

### Adapt or adopt?

I called Sue, a young 16-year-old girl, into my vestry one day. She'd looked sad in the meeting and I wanted to see if there was anything wrong. She explained that her mother and step-father were emigrating to Australia and she didn't want to go. She wasn't a Christian but was involved with the Mission. She was courting a young man called Terry and did not want to lose him. And she wanted to keep her job.

I told her that if she ended up with nowhere to stay, Grace and I would be happy for her to live with us. It was one of those emotional moments when you say things you later regret. And regret it, I did!

It wasn't long before her angry mother was banging on our front door. 'What do you think you are doing?' she exploded as she marched into the house.

'What do you mean?' I asked, bewildered by this full-on attack.

'Sue says she doesn't have to go to Australia, because Norman and Grace will look after her! What on earth gives you the right to interfere in our family life? I am trying to keep the family together, and here you are, doing exactly the opposite.'

I could only eat humble pie and apologise.

Around the same time, my brother-in-law, who worked for Social Services, asked us to foster a young girl. We were reluctant – we'd tried to adopt, but were turned down because of our age difference, our low income, and because we didn't own our own home. We had considered fostering, but felt unable to cope with the emotional turmoil of caring for a child and then having to say goodbye. But this was long-term fostering. So we agreed.

The day before we were due to sign the fostering papers, a lady in our church phoned Grace. At the end of the conversation, she made a chance remark. 'I hear you are going to have a young girl living with you!'

'Oh, yes,' said Grace, thinking of the girl we were about to foster.

'Susan's mum told me that you're having Susan to live with you.'

Grace couldn't believe her ears. Now it was my turn to bang on Sue's front door to ask her mother what was going on!

'Oh yes,' she said, 'we thought it was a good idea and decided to take you up on your offer.'

So we cancelled the plan to foster and Sue moved in with us.

## Our family begins

The first year was hard – we all had to adapt. We suddenly had a teenage girl thrust on us, with all the problems that can bring. And Sue had to get used to our hectic lifestyle, which was different to anything she had known. You should never underestimate the difficulties involved in extended families!

We didn't pressure Sue to become a Christian. We just encouraged her to be part of our lives, and after talking to us over a period of time, she began to trust us.

The year after she moved in, something remarkable happened in the Mission's Bible class, which comprised around 25 young people. One Sunday God gave me a prophetic word for each member of the group.

The next day, Sue came home from work, and was very quiet. We realised that God was speaking to her. The following evening, she came to us and said, 'I've sorted it out. I want to become a Christian. Terry doesn't want to become a Christian, but I'm leaving that with him. I want to go on with God.'

Within a day or two, Terry contacted us and told us that he wanted to become a Christian too. So we had the joy of leading them both to the Lord. Our spiritual family had started.

The following Sunday they gave their testimonies and over the next month, 20 young people were saved, baptised and filled with the Holy Spirit. We suddenly had more 'sons and daughters' than we knew what to do with.

Sue lived with us for three years, and became like a daughter to us. We helped to pay for her wedding and it was a joy when she and her husband Terry moved in almost opposite us.

Before long, Sue became pregnant with Stephanie. Someone in the church asked Sue where Grace and I would fit into the picture when Stephanie was born. 'Of course,' said Sue, in all naivety, 'they can choose what they want to be called, Nana and Grandpa, or Grandma and Grandad.' She had already counted us in! So we became Grandma and Grandad to little Stephanie. And our connection with Sue and Terry didn't end there. Sue had trouble falling pregnant with her second child, so we all prayed and fasted one day a week for five years. And eventually God answered, and Stephanie's brother, Paul, was born.

## A son is given

We had asked God for children and He had answered our prayers, far beyond what we expected. But something still niggled me. So after some deliberation I brought the matter before the Lord.

'Could I please have a son to carry on my name?' I asked. It was a ridiculous and impossible request, but by this time I felt so strongly about it, that I could do nothing else but pursue it with God.

In the 21st century Western world, we place very little value on names. But in Biblical times a child's name was hugely significant. It still is in certain cultures today. It may reflect character, or the parents' dreams for him or her. Or it may signify ties with family, tribe or community.

Having a son to carry on the family name has lost some of its value in the West. Maybe it makes women seem less important. In some parts of the world, women are still regarded as second class citizens because they don't carry their family name once they are married.

In 1980, Daniel, an elder from the church in Kwadaso, came to England and stayed a month with Grace and me. Mindful of the hospitality I had received in Ghana, we treated him like royalty. We bought him clothes and helped him to choose clothes for his wife, Mary, and paid for those, too.

In 1981 we visited Ghana again and David Mills approached us. 'Norman and Grace, you've got a problem,' he said.

'Oh, what's that?' we replied.

'Daniel and Mary have been talking. They were so blessed by the way you looked after Daniel when he was in England, they want to give you a gift.'

We were deeply moved by the generosity of this couple who had so little, yet were willing to sacrifice everything to bless us. But nothing could have prepared us for what David said next.

'Because you have no children of your own, they would like to give you their youngest son.'

We could hardly take in what we'd heard. It took our breath away. We knew that this was not just a gesture, but a serious offer, especially coming from Ghanaians, who hold their children very dear. We were reduced to tears – not for the first time in our travels to Ghana.

Ghanaian law prevented us from taking the boy back home. And I doubt if we would have done so anyway. Although we were overwhelmed by the enormity of the gift, we could not have taken the child away from his culture and his surroundings. So we left him in Ghana, but Grace and I echoed Isaiah's words: 'To us a son is given.'

Some time after we got back to England, we received a letter from Daniel. 'Your son is doing well. His name was Ebenezer, but now he is old enough to understand, he wishes to be called Norman Barnes. That is now his adopted name.'

My prayers for a son to bear my family name had been answered. We cried a lot. And it didn't stop there ...

## What's in a name?

Later we heard that Nicholas Andoh's wife had given birth to a son – and they had decided to call him Norman Barnes, too! And Grace wasn't left out. The wife of Johnny, another of the elders in Kwadaso, had a little girl. Now in Ghana, they traditionally name children after people they wish to honour, and the couple were under pressure to name her after her grandmother. But Johnny flatly refused. The grandmother was dead, and he did not want his daughter named after a dead person. He wanted to name her after somebody he honoured and who was alive.

'I want to call my little daughter after Mammy Barnes,' he declared. He wanted to honour the way that Grace, a white woman, had gone to Ghana and showed them love, care and concern. It was moving for Grace, especially when she heard the name Grace Barnes given to the little girl at her dedication.

So God heard our cries and gave us nephews and nieces, children and grandchildren, and three little Africans named after us. Over the years we paid for their education – what a great way to invest your money! Now one of the Normans – Mark Two – is an engineering surveyor and Grace Mark Two has a management degree. We're so proud of them and couldn't love them more if they were our own.

Later on, John and Chris Norton were expecting another child. One evening after the little boy was born, as we all sat around the tea table, John said, 'We have decided on a name for the baby. We are going to call him Simon.'

'That's nice,' I replied.

'But we want to give him another name – Barnes. We would like to call him Simon Barnes Norton. We want him to have your name because of our relationship and close friendship, and when he grows up, I'll explain to him why.'

Once again, we were moved to tears by the kindness of our friends – and of God Himself.

## Blessings, but …

I have to say, though, that all these blessings and miracles never compensated for the fact that we did not have our own children. We still cannot fully understand why God did not bless us with them. But with God, there are things we don't know and shouldn't know. Being childless freed us to travel, give more time to the Lord, look after children from broken homes and serve parents in the Church. But nothing will ever fill the void in our hearts – we still live with the pain today. We used to get hurt hearing parents talking about their children. Now we still hurt when grandparents talk about their grandchildren. If we could re-run history, we would choose to have children every time. But God does give you the grace to cope – not a one-off 'zap', but something you draw on continually, minute by minute and day by day. It's not easy, when you're hurting so deeply.

## Getting our own back!

Grace and I have often found that people are powerfully impacted when we pray for them to have children. Sometimes God gives us prophetic words for them, telling them to trust Him for children. In fact God has given Grace a precious ministry in praying for childless women.

In February 1997, we visited Bridge Church in Brentford, and Dr Patrick Dixon asked couples to come forward if they were unable to conceive. Twelve responded. Grace prayed for them, and at the last count, ten of the wives were pregnant!

She also prayed for a childless couple at Grapevine in August 2007 – and by April 2008 the lady had received a 'double portion' … she was pregnant with twins!

Remarkably, we are always able to rejoice with these expectant parents, without feeling resentment or jealousy. I guess that's because of the healing God has brought to our lives. But it doesn't mean we don't feel the pain of not having our own children, and sometimes we get very emotional. But there is a difference between hurting and weeping and becoming bitter and hard. Hurting and weeping bring healing … and God promises to keep our tears in a bottle. Every tear-drop is precious to Him.

People often ask why God uses Grace like this. We believe we're stepping on the enemy's neck. If we can't have children, then we'll help to extend God's Kingdom by praying for others to have them instead!

### Better or bitter?

Our prayers for people to have children aren't always answered.

We are sometimes asked to help other couples who are struggling with the grim reality of childlessness. We try to pass on what we've learned as we continue to walk through that black valley of despair. In the absence of longed-for children, we have seen God fill that emptiness in people's hearts time and again. He reaches those tender places that no human being could ever reach.

We usually tell people things that have helped us. They have to make the right choices. Scripture says, 'I *will* rejoice.' That's a decision. Childlessness can make you bitter, and that's something Grace and I have had to guard against over the years. We all live with our choices, both the right ones and the wrong ones.

It's so sad when you see childless people become hard-hearted and bitter. It's as if the enemy has scored a double victory. So we encourage people to praise God in their pain and to keep their hearts soft. God allows tears, because they are an emotion. But bitterness is an attitude – and one that we must resist.

It helps if we can embrace the truth of Psalm 16 – that God has drawn our boundary lines in pleasant places. They may not seem pleasant to us – but we have to trust that God has drawn them for our good, even if we cannot understand why and it seems thoroughly unfair.

Jacob had to embrace Leah before he received Rachel as his wife. He was deceived into marrying the wrong woman – totally unjust. Where was God in that? But when he embraced the situation, with all the pain, injustice and frustration involved, God gave him his heart's desire.

Once I heard God speak to me about our situation. 'Son, I have more than one way of answering prayer,' He said.

That promise is as true for you as it is for us. Pain is often part of the dreamer's job description. But when we sow in tears, we will reap with joy.

# CHAPTER 9

# THE LAND
# OF DREAMS

## Our American dream

We were in a plane high above the Atlantic, flying towards the USA. Our destination was still several hours away. We had eaten a good meal and had settled down for the rest of the journey. It was October 2008, just before the Presidential election. And as I sat on the plane, quietly gazing out of the window, I began to reflect on the dozens of trips Grace and I had made to America over the years. I love the USA. The lifestyle and culture sit well with my outgoing personality and love of action.

For many people, America is the land of dreams. The Statue of Liberty is a great symbol of freedom. We often hear about people pursuing the 'American dream'. And millions enjoy the nation's prosperity – though this has brought problems as well as blessings. And of course, that prosperity is not for everyone.

God placed a dream in my heart for America back in the 1960s. I'd read books and seen films about some of the great men of faith – people like T. L. Osborn, Kenneth Hagan and Oral Roberts. But it was different to the dream I had about Ghana. I was keen to see what God was doing there, and I wanted to meet people who had experienced the exciting move of the Holy Spirit.

But I will always be grateful that God took me to Ghana before America. It's important to remember that two-thirds of the world live like Ghanaians – not like Americans. And although I enjoy our trips to America, Africa is a constant reminder that most people on earth live in serious need.

## A leap of faith

We've been going to the USA three times a year for the past 15 years now. We usually visit four churches during each trip. We only work relationally, so we tend to go back to the same churches and only visit new ones if they come out of an existing friendship. We're always getting new invitations – far more than we can cope with now we're trying to slow down a bit in our retirement!

A typical trip lasts around 21 days. The churches plan our itinerary – we're in other people's hands as to where we go and what we do. We stay in a mixture of houses and hotels, and usually arrive at the right place at the right time, and hopefully with the right words.

Over the years, we've visited churches in Texas, Oklahoma, Michigan, Indiana, Florida, and other states, too. And we've covered a whole range of denominations – Baptists, Assemblies of God, faith churches and independent charismatic churches. That's the great thing about working out of friendships – you are able to cover a whole range of groups.

Some people think we only go to America for the money. But that's far from the truth. We always pay our own fares – around $4,000 a time – and we never ask for money up front as some ministries do. In fact we don't ask for anything. We never want money to be an issue for any church we visit. Some places give us little or nothing – others give us more. And we often find when we get home that we've just about broken even or have a bit to spare. More importantly we've enjoyed fun and friendship and seen people blessed and encouraged. You can't put a price tag on that. People often gasp at the accuracy of the prophetic words that God gives us. Some even thought I might be using my hearing aids as radio receivers to obtain 'words of knowledge' about people, like Steve Martin did in *Leap of Faith*! I think I'd find it easier to hear God!

## Pioneering is infectious!

As we journeyed back to America for the 40th time, I realised that this nation's pioneering spirit had touched my own heart.

You don't always realise the significance of what you are doing at the time. But we found ourselves trying something new almost every time we went – things we wouldn't have done in England. And we certainly helped to break the mould at some of the churches we visited.

But that's what America's like. They pioneer all the time, whether it's putting a man on the moon or having a black president. They think big. They have faith and are prepared to take risks. They find reasons why things *can* be done. In the UK we tend to do the opposite!

One of our early visits was to a church in Russellville, Arkansas. We had been asked to speak at one of their meetings, which were usually quite short. But I was convinced that God wanted to do something different, and asked the leader for more time. He looked a bit surprised!

As I began to speak about dreams and visions, people started to weep. Then we felt compelled to go to certain couples and prophesy over them. It was a real step of faith – we'd never done anything like that before. But we were keen to pioneer, even though we were scared stiff! Some of the things we said were very precise, and people's reactions showed we must have heard God correctly.

One couple believed the Lord was going to test their faith by taking their baby away from them. We stood with them against this lie.

We were also able to prophesy to six widows about their future ministries. We carried on ministering to people even after the meeting closed, bringing them words of prophecy and encouragement.

We were amazed as we laid hands on people that the Holy Spirit gave us words of knowledge. Once again, we had pioneered something in this land of pioneers – and God had blessed us and other people, too. Having a 'short meeting' didn't come into it!

When we got back to England, someone we prayed for wrote and told us, 'You will never know what a comfort your ministry was to me. If it was not for your word I would have gone insane, due to the difficulties I was facing at the time.' Pioneering is scary. But the rewards are immense.

## Washing feet with tears ...

We left Russellville and travelled to Little Rock, another town in Arkansas, to spend time with an old friend called Peter Parris. He had arranged a retreat for five leaders and me. During the night I woke up and sensed the Holy Spirit tell me I should wash the other men's feet. 'But Lord,' I protested, 'that's ridiculous. It has absolutely no cultural relevance.'

I continued to protest, and then said to the Lord, 'Well, I am not going around looking for a bucket and that's final. There is no bowl in the sink because they use dishwashers.'

I really thought I'd played my ace card. But then my eyes went to the corner of the room – and there in all its glory was a wash stand with an old-fashioned pitcher and basin. My heart sank, but so did my will! I knew when I was beaten. Then God began to give me some prophetic words to speak to the other leaders as I drifted back to sleep.

Next morning, Peter Parris asked me as he cooked breakfast, 'What are we going to do today, Norman?'

I told him, with some embarrassment, 'I want to use the pitcher and washbasin to wash your feet. I don't understand what it means – it has no relevance to me, but I feel strongly that this is what God wants me to do.'

So the 'meeting' started, and I went to Peter with the washbasin and a towel in my hands. After kneeling in front of him, I removed his shoes and socks. 'I feel such a fool,' was all I could say. I was thoroughly embarrassed. But I rinsed his feet and dried them, praying and speaking in tongues as I did so. Well, what else was I supposed to do?

As I got to the second man, I was struck by the reality of what I was doing. The picture of Jesus washing the disciples' feet came into sharp focus and I was reduced to tears. By the time I reached the third man, I could have washed his feet with them! My eyes were like fountains. I sobbed uncontrollably. I could hardly see because they were so swollen. Then I staggered to the last man, but couldn't kneel or stand. I collapsed in an emotional heap on the floor. Somehow I managed to drag myself up and wash his feet and then I tried to move towards my chair. But I couldn't get up to sit! So I knelt beside it and sobbed the deepest sobs I have ever known.

We all realised God had revealed the truth about laying down our lives for our friends. I did not feel humiliated, just deeply humbled.

In those brief moments I saw Jesus, the Son of God as the Son of Man, emptying Himself of all His glory to become a servant saviour. I felt so unworthy. To say I had mixed emotions would be an understatement!

Then the other men gathered round me and washed my feet – and they were reduced to tears, too. I began to pray and had a word that was very relevant to each person. It was a precious time, marked by God's healing presence.

## Healing relationships

Later on, we received an invitation to visit the home of a prophetic couple called Charles and Paula Slagle and speak on community, covenant relationships and commitment.

My first stop was a prayer breakfast in the town of Azle, near Fort Worth. There was plenty of good humour, and after an enormous American breakfast, I was asked to speak to the men. I spoke about the qualities of leadership and was aware of a hush descending on the gathering. The Holy Spirit was stirring these men. It was a good start to the trip.

On the Sunday I shared about covenant relationships, using Ruth and Naomi, and David and Jonathan as examples. Then Grace and I prayed for people, and prophesied over them. We spoke to one family who were apparently backslidden. Through a word of knowledge we were able to describe how God saw the man's relationship with his wife and children. The man broke like a bursting dam. Healing had begun.

Then we prayed for a young couple whom we sensed were going through a tough time. They began to cry. I also felt I should prophesy to a man in the congregation, and told him that God was going to exalt him, even though he had been through a very low time. Little did I know that he had been a millionaire, but his business had gone bust. Then I suddenly realised that the husband of the young couple I had just spoken to was this man's son. 'God wants you two to be reconciled,' I said. 'There needs to be a renewing of your relationship.' I brought the father and son together and before long, they were weeping on each other's shoulders.

I also sensed the relationship between the wife and mother-in-law needed healing, so I brought them together, too. It was a very moving moment to see the four of them sobbing in the aisle together. There was hardly a dry eye in the place.

We prophesied over many people that day, both young and old, with the same results every time. People broke down and wept as they were reconciled to one another and to God. We spent four nights in Azle, and every time was the same. Sometimes the hush of the Holy Spirit descended on the meeting like a gentle breeze. No one dared move. It was quite remarkable how God blessed His people that week.

## Real friendship

On the last day, Kerry Wood, the Pastor of the church in Azle, asked me to speak to the leaders. We met at 6am for another breakfast session. Kerry asked me, 'Please tell us about the cost of the relationships you have been talking about.'

I spoke about the hurts that are inevitable in any serious relationship. There would always be misunderstandings, mistakes and miscommunication. As I spoke, I was moved to see these men with a genuine hunger for God and a real desire to learn.

'Once you have seen the blessing that committed relationships bring,' I told them, 'nothing less will satisfy you. You won't be able to go back and accept superficial involvement with people any more.'

Some of these pastors didn't have any deep, lasting friendships. They were placed on a pedestal by the congregation, given a title of 'Pastor', and expected to live an almost perfect life. There was no place for them to share their weaknesses or vulnerabilities ... and no one, apart from their marriage partners, to share their problems with. If they made special friends, it could be seen as favouritism. Many of them were trying to bear a burden which God never intended them to carry on their own. Many were desperate for deep friendships.

By the time I had finished, we were all weeping. That day we got a glimpse of the joy, as well as the hurts, that true, committed relationships can bring. And we thanked God that we were part of the same family – and that by pursuing covenant relationships, we would see Christ revealed in the Church.

## Pastors need fathers

There's a real shortage of father figures in American churches, and there isn't much in the way of apostolic covering either. Pastors who run a church with 1,000 members don't often relate to pastors with a church of 100. And most relationships are professional – a bit like you'd have in the secular world.

The leaders we visit see us as friends – and we couldn't operate any other way. We offer ourselves, our friendship, our popcorn and our pizza – and see what God will do. Some leaders have told us they would have quit the ministry had it not been for our input – they find there's very little help available.

Many pastors in the USA live under the permanent shadow of the mega-ministries and the TV evangelists. And sadly, the divide between the two is getting bigger. So the church scene in America is becoming an enigma: the number of church-goers is declining, but the nation is home to some of the largest churches in the world.

## Ordinary pioneers

A lot of Americans found it hard to work us out. They'd never seen 'ministers' like us before! We placed a big emphasis on relationships, the core of everything we do. But this is unusual in the USA.

They're also more used to 'The Prophet' or 'The Apostle' coming through, whereas we were just Norman and Grace from Dagenham, UK, and we weren't sure whether we were prophets, apostles or something else besides! We run a mile from being the 'big name preachers' – you're more likely to find us watching a DVD and eating popcorn with a church's leader than being super-spiritual with them. It's who we are that matters, not what titles we have. We're their friends. And we're just as happy to go to small churches as large ones. There are no strings attached – we're never out to 'cover them' or 'own them'. We just want to be with them, and they want to be with us.

Many churches in the States have given us an open invitation to go and speak whenever we're passing through. But to be honest, we'd be just as happy to visit them and not speak!

## The same – but different

Our ministry in America has been fruitful because we went out of our way to learn the culture. It's completely different from ours. Many folk assume that because we speak the same language and wear the same clothes, then we are the same. But everything's different – American values, attitudes, habits. We found it easier to relate to Ghanaian culture than American.

## Good news to the rich?

So how does this fit in with Links? Some people find it hard to understand how we can minister to the richest nation on earth –

and to some of the poorest. But Grace and I don't see any contradiction. We believe we are missionaries to the United States, just the same as we are missionaries to Ghana. Some people can't cope with that – and in some ways, it doesn't make much sense. But by faith, it works. We don't find it difficult to embrace the dire poverty in Africa and the American teaching about sowing, reaping and faith.

We still feel a huge burden for America. Even though we've cut down on our travelling, we still have a strong desire to continue our work there. We believe we're called to both the rich and the poor. Poverty never glorifies God – unless someone has chosen it, as Mother Theresa did. But excessive riches don't glorify God, either. They're both as bad as each other.

You tend to find that Christians either have a perception of a 'poor' Jesus, or a 'rich' one. They adapt him to suit their own values and cultures. But the Jesus that Grace and I read about was equally happy talking to priests and prostitutes ... dining with Sadducees and sinners ... preaching to elders and evil-doers. Who are we to do any different?

It's all about people – rich people, poor people, black people and white people, good people and bad people. People are so important to God ... important enough to die for. Whatever our dreams are, people will always matter the most.

# CHAPTER 10

# INDIA – FRUSTRATION AND FASCINATION

### Welcome to Delhi!

I'd spent two hours being shunted back and forth between different enquiry desks and was getting nowhere. I was fast becoming fed up with Delhi Airport. I'd lost an item of luggage – the one thing that every air traveller dreads!

My plane had landed at Delhi airport around the same time as three other jumbo jets, so luggage belonging to around 1,200 people cascaded onto the carousels all at once. There was a mad rush. Nobody knew which belt their luggage was on, and people pushed and shoved everyone else, regardless of age or gender.

Eventually I gave up. I was even beginning to slightly regret applying to the Shaftesbury Society for a £1,500 grant to cover a three month sabbatical. But then I reasoned I'd be back in a week's time and could hopefully collect the missing case then. So I headed for the Customs Hall.

There, I was asked if I had a Customs Declaration form. Of course, I hadn't got one. So I queued, yet again, at the appropriate desk, but the official was very reluctant to give me one. Then the penny dropped – or should I say the rupee! I hadn't paid a 'tip' to speed things up. By this time I was tired, frustrated, hot and very angry, and I told the official in no uncertain terms I wasn't going to pay him. He handed me the form, with the smile still intact on his face and his politeness seemingly unruffled! I guess that came with years of practice.

## Contrasts everywhere

Ian Farr, my long time friend from Yeovil, was waiting for me. After three hours I was thoroughly relieved to leave the airport. But as we drove off, India's extraordinary contrasts began to hit me. One moment a gleaming Mercedes flashed by ... followed by a rickshaw and then a camel cart. I was struck by the teeming masses of people – thousands of them were riding bikes. There were Hindu shrines on every street corner and even in every taxi. They ranged from ant hills to buildings more than 100 feet tall. Cows wandered the streets – and if you accidentally hit one, you got out and ran for your life!

I couldn't help comparing India with Ghana. There was more food in the shops in India, yet the people looked poorer. For every one unkempt person I had seen in Ghana, there were hundreds in India.

We stayed the night with a local pastor and returned to the airport next day to fly north to Dehra Dun airport, a tarmac strip in the middle of nowhere with tents for buildings. Security was very tight because of the tension between Sikhs and Hindus. I had to remove my shoes and socks and let them inspect the bottom of my feet! Little did I know that similar measures would be introduced at UK airports 20 years later. That was unthinkable here back in the 1980s.

We took a hair-raising 60 kilometre taxi ride to get to the Farrs' home in Mussoorie. We spent most of the journey praying for a safe arrival! All that mattered on the road was size. If you drove a

40 ton truck, you were king. The smaller your vehicle, the less important you were, right down to the pedestrians, who were definitely the lowest of the low.

When we arrived, we had to lug our heavy bags up a steep, rocky path to Ian's house. It was like climbing a ladder! But we made it. Mussoorie was in the Himalayan foothills, 7,500 feet above sea level. The view from the Farrs' house took your breath away – it was one of the most beautiful spots in India. The hills and fields shimmered in the sunshine and looked like a picture from a book. But poverty surrounded me. It didn't seem right, set against such beauty.

## Such as they had …

That afternoon we visited an orphanage in Mussoorie, run by an Indian couple called Swami and Pami. They presented me with a garland of flowers and showed me round. Each child had a tin plate and cup, but very few other possessions. By Indian standards they were fairly well dressed and cared for, and received a good education. But in the West we would have taken their beds straight down the dump. It made me cry.

The home was rundown due to lack of funds. Swami and Pami had originally been sponsored by a group of Christians in the West, but their cash was cut off when they came into a charismatic experience. So adults argued about theology – and children suffered as a result. Swami and Pami had nothing, but gave us a lovely meal of curried buffalo meat!

When we had finished, I shared the scripture from Acts 3, 'What I have I give you'. I told them they may not have any rupees, but they did have Jesus, and could share Him with others. We prayed for Swami and Pami and gathered the children round them to bless their adopted mum and dad. Everyone cried. I prophesied to Swami that he would learn to weep himself. I was told later my comments had confirmed what God had been saying to him directly. That was a real encouragement.

As a result of that visit, Links International gave the home £500, with the promise of a further £500 later on. I was so blessed that God had opened up a way for us to help people who badly needed assistance.

Ian and Gwen Farr's children both went to Woodstock, an international school for children whose parents were Europeans and Americans working in India. One evening we were invited to speak to a group of about 25 of the staff, all Christians. I spoke and prophesied over around seven or so of them – very direct, detailed and encouraging words. People wept and were obviously blessed by God.

## Not for shirts and trousers!

Two weeks earlier, I'd mentioned my forthcoming trip at a conference in Nottingham. A man came up to me afterwards and said that I was not to go to India 'for shirts and trousers' – which is how he described relief work. I was to go and confidently speak the word of the Lord. I was used to preaching, so I have to admit I didn't take a great deal of notice. But his words turned out to be more significant than I realised.

Almost a month later, I woke up at about 3am and God spoke to me about Woodstock School Christian Union, where I was speaking again the following evening. He gave me vivid prophetic words for people that were still fresh in my mind in the morning. He also told me to use props with each word, to make them more realistic. I was worried. I'd never done anything like that before.

That evening I spoke on my favourite theme, Dreams and Visions, and as I did so, the Holy Spirit started to touch people in a very significant way. So I decided to give the prophetic words, starting with Ian Farr. I went to him and placed a blanket over his head. I think he reckoned I'd finally lost it!

But then I said to him, 'You've been hidden for a while, but the day of your appearing is near.' Ian just burst into tears. I found out later that this helped to launch him into a much wider ministry.

Then I went to a woman, held her hand and asked for the light to be turned out for a few seconds – not my usual style with women I've never met before, I can assure you! By now, I was worried I was making a complete fool of myself. I think this lady was, too! But I pressed on, and told her, 'I'm as embarrassed about this as you are! But God has told me to do this. Please turn the light back on.' I looked at her.

'Did you notice before the light went out that I was holding your hand?' I asked.

'Yes,' she said.

'The light is back on again – and I'm still holding your hand. God says that He will never leave you, even though you have felt darkness in your spirit. He will never let you go.' She was reduced to tears.

I turned to another couple. 'I see you with babies in your arms,' I told them.

'Oh, no,' they groaned. 'We don't want any more!' Hardly encouraging, but I pressed on.

'No, God is going to birth new things in and through you. A new day is dawning.' I found out later they were about to leave the school to start a new work.

Then I said to another couple, 'I see a word over you. It is "security". There is a security about your relationship that blesses people. God wants you to teach others about marriage.'

They looked astounded. 'We're no different from anyone else!' they said. But everyone in the room burst out laughing. It was obvious that they had a good marriage and gave out a lot more than they realised.

I also had words for people who weren't present, so the next day I went around the campus looking for them. I went to an American couple's house and asked everyone to hold hands. Then I said, 'You are a part of the body of Christ and are not separated from everyone else. You have been more effective than you realise. By holding hands together, the Lord wants to show you what friendship is all about.'

I also found a New Zealander called Geoff. 'The Lord has told me to wash your feet,' I told him.

'No, no, I can't cope with that,' he protested. But I just got on with it – I was becoming an old 'hand' at 'feet' by now! 'The Lord wants to honour you in this way because you have so willingly laid down your life for others,' I told him.

'I can't see how,' he replied.

'God's word for you is, "I was hungry and you gave me something to eat, I was thirsty and you gave me something to drink. I was a stranger and you invited me in, I needed clothes and you clothed me, I was sick and you looked after me, I was in prison and you came to visit me."'

'When have I done that?' he asked, genuinely astounded. It was almost a replay of the words from Matthew 25. So I answered directly from that scripture. 'Whatever you did for one of the least of these brothers of mine, you did for me.'

Ian later confirmed that Geoff opened up his home to just about everybody, and failed to realise how much God appreciated his servant heart.

I felt elated and deeply satisfied. If I had come to India only to experience this development of my ministry, the trip would have been worthwhile – even though it was scary at times!

## Orphans, orphans, and more orphans

Orphanages are one of the major growth industries in India. What a tragedy.

Nothing touches your emotions more than children who have lost their parents. They look so disorientated, isolated, bewildered and drained of hope. Thank God for the organisations who provide them with a home, food and education – and a life-changing relationship with Jesus.

Many parents abandon their children because they can't afford to feed them. Imagine their despair. They are distraught and grieved, the same as we would be. During our first trip to India, we visited a number of orphanages … and our hearts were broken time and time again.

When you are confronted with such pain and sadness, it's easy to make an emotional response, rather than do what's best. I was often reminded how Jesus refused to let His emotions rule His decision-making when His close friend, Lazarus, died. His heart may well have wanted to rush straight over. But He stayed in tune with God, and turned up four days 'late'.

Our hearts certainly ruled our heads and we just provided money and equipment the best we could. And many children's needs were met by the kindness of people back in the UK and beyond. But we began to realise that support like this made orphanages dependent on us, and didn't solve the underlying poverty. So we faced a different challenge – how to make them self-sufficient. Our focus had to change.

Over the years, with God's help, we've been involved in pioneering initiatives that have worked towards changing the lives of children who have been given the worst possible start in life.

### Success stories

We began examining how we could make orphanages self-sustaining. It wasn't always possible. But we have seen some remarkable success stories.

We asked working adults who grew up in an orphanage to give money to the homes that brought them up. And we encouraged Indian people to sponsor orphans rather than rely on donations from the UK. There *was* money available, and still is. It's a very rich country and it's better if Indian children are supported by their own communities.

We're not knocking organisations that encourage child sponsorship – we have sponsors at Links who play a big part in children's lives. But we aim to end the dependence on the West that will never allow this nation and its people to flourish and find their potential.

We also helped to arrange training programmes so that orphans could earn a living. The boys learn carpentry, engineering and plumbing and the girls study computers and how to operate machinery. To begin with, the training takes place informally, in the orphanages. But when the children are older, they go to a vocational school or day college and eventually get jobs. So the poverty cycle is broken.

I remember once meeting a well dressed and prosperous young businessman in the Sheraton Hotel in Chennai. He used to live in one of our orphanages. What a transformation! Over the years, we have seen hundreds of young people released from a childhood of hopelessness into an adult life of relative prosperity and fulfilment.

One hotel provided work experience for four teenage girls from a training school. The manager, whose usual practice was to employ graduates from university, was so impressed by their work ethic, honesty and integrity that he gave them jobs! Opportunities like this give young people dignity, self worth, and the chance to do well in a society that had written them off before they could walk or talk.

The 'mini-loans' I described earlier in this book also helped people in this vast continent. In the past, a mum would put her son into care because she couldn't afford to feed him. But now we lend her the money to start a business, so she can keep her family together. This approach has borne fruit hundreds of times.

We also moved away from institutional orphanages, and established families, where 'mum and dad' live with 12 children and care for them as if they are their own. Deep friendships are born, and the children enjoy a far more secure and happier start in life. They are taught how to live and how to love, rather than simply how to survive. It's the least that God's children deserve. He takes the lonely and places them in families – not in institutions!

## The dream-like continent

It didn't take long to recognise the grip that Hinduism has on India. There were shrines and temples everywhere I went. People's bodies and minds were controlled by this suppressive religion and their lives determined by the wicked caste system. Hinduism's fatalistic doctrine doesn't allow people any hope of improving their lives. If you are a road-sweeper, you will always be a road-sweeper and your children will be road-sweepers, too. Your 'karma' seals your fate, and you can't change it. What a contrast with the life-changing hope that Jesus offers!

I watched, with a mixture of pity and anger, as people worshipped trees, anthills and stone gods and tried to purify themselves in pools of filthy water. They were locked into a dream-like, hopeless existence. It was a challenge when I first went to India – and still is.

Hindus who become Christians encounter huge problems. They are often thrown out of their homes and cut off from their families, which is especially traumatic because Hindu families are very closely knit.

Some parents go to amazing lengths to persuade a Christian son or daughter to renounce their new faith in Jesus. They resort to bribery, and even arrange a marriage as a trap. Some new converts who are under 18 have to believe in secret while they are dependent on their parents for support.

## A light in the darkness

Down in India's south-eastern corner is an island called Rameswaram, one of the main Hindu centres. The whole island is a shrine and every Hindu dreams of visiting it. We went there, and I was immediately impacted by the spiritual darkness. People's faces were etched with utter despair. There were hundreds of shrines of all shapes and sizes. Some were no bigger than mounds of earth. Others were huge.

There were extremes of poverty and wealth, again the result of the awful doctrine of karma and the caste system. Beggars abounded.

But strutting alongside them were the high-caste Bramin, with cords hanging over their bare shoulders. This was the evidence of their caste, and they never removed them, even when they were bathing.

Living in the middle of this darkness was a diminutive man called Paulose who had dared to challenge the might of Hinduism. God told him to take his wife and children to the island to preach the Gospel. They had nowhere to live, no money and couldn't speak the language. But he found two rooms to live in, put his children into the school and set about his task.

Ian Farr and I spent two days with Paulose and his lovely, simple family. They treated us to a delicious meal in their tiny home and showed us genuine hospitality. Paulose had been trained by Operation Mobilisation and had a clear apostolic call from God.

I discovered that he had established a church of approximately 40 believers and another group of 30 in a nearby fishing village. He also discipled a group of eight men and sent them out every day to preach the Gospel. They were often spat at, beaten up and stoned. When I asked Paulose why they carried on in the face of such opposition, he answered simply: 'We love Jesus.'

He might have been small, but he was a mighty man of faith who knew God and His supernatural power. Once he went to a village to preach, and the villagers tied him to a tree and tried to skin him alive. They failed, but beat him up and left him for dead instead. He escaped, however, and made it home where he asked God to heal his injuries, so he could return to complete his preaching mission! God healed him, and when he arrived back at the village, the tree he had been tied to was *dead*! The villagers were terrified at this display of God's power and many turned to Christ. Paulose was a man of love, but I was glad to be working with him and not against him!

His church had a vision to build a place to worship God on the island. When we first went there, the Lord had already given them a plot of land, and as we write this, we've heard they have nearly finished building a Bible school. Now that's what I call spiritual warfare … setting up God's HQ right in the middle of the enemy's turf! It reminded me of Paul preaching on Mars Hill in Acts 17. He took the battle to the devil in one of the main centres of idolatry. Far more effective than bellowing at the devil in a church prayer meeting with the doors safely closed!

Paulose has now planted churches in other parts of the island. And he continues to see miracles through his courage and devotion to God. When the tsunami struck the area in 2006, he called his church together for prayer … and the waves went *round* the island. Lives and property were saved. Then his church gave food and other essentials to survivors in other areas, and gained great favour as a result. What a fine display of God's power and love working together.

Another time, God told Paulose to buy a plot of land, where he discovered fresh water. So he dug a well and released precious supplies … streams in the desert, just like Isaiah prophesied.

The local Hindu priests don't like Paulose. But they can't ignore him … or his God. And they certainly cannot deny the love, power and character that he displays!

### Filth and fashion

During that first trip to India, a guy named James Roxborough, of New Life Fellowship in Mumbai (formerly Bombay), took us to Slum City – the worst slum in Asia. It was hell on earth. The smell was sickening and revolting – I'd never experienced anything like it. Refuse was piled two feet high. There was dirt, filth, open drains, human excrement, sick dogs, dead cats, rats, and millions of flies. And yet people lived and worked there. The city comprised huts of various shapes and sizes separated by alleyways three to four feet wide. A 12ft x 14ft hut cost between 25,000 to 30,000 rupees – about £2,000. There was no water or sanitation.

But right in the middle of the filth and squalor stood a small church where 150 people crammed in to worship the living God.

Wherever we travelled, we couldn't escape the stark contrast between rich and poor. The modern hotels and blocks of flats stood proudly on the waterfront, shining examples of the luxury and wealth available to the few. But in their shadows stood the grim straw huts where the poor people lived.

Once, we went for a walk on a beach near Mumbai. You could have been anywhere in the world. There were well dressed Indian families in carriages, on horse-back, having pony rides, enjoying the fun fair and buying food. But you didn't have to go far to find the poor, struggling to eke out a meagre and pitiful existence.

## Same-day abortions

Another time, while travelling by train in Mumbai, I saw a poster which advertised, 'Abortions 70 rupees – 2 hours and back to work'. My heart sank. I was horrified to think that a human life could be extinguished for less than £5. Contraception doesn't play a major part in Indian family life.

I learned that when Sanjay Gandhi was alive, he introduced a programme of enforced sterilisation. Soldiers would surround a village and force the men to have vasectomies. The men fled to the foothills when they heard soldiers approaching.

## Health and safety

I certainly sampled some unusual food while I was in India! During a trip from Mussoorie to Nainital, we stopped at a little place on the roadside. None of us had eaten breakfast so we were pretty hungry. I could see bread on the counter, but I decided to give it a miss when I noticed the corners had been nibbled by rats! I always played it safe with food, so I settled for some boiled eggs that were hanging up in wire baskets. After all, I reasoned, they were in shells and I could peel them myself – they must be safe.

But I didn't reckon on the kindness of the gentleman who served me. He'd obviously been on a customer care course! Instead of handing the egg to me in its shell, he cracked it, peeled it with both hands, and then handed it to me covered in dirty, sweaty, fingerprints. I was really hungry, so I said a quick prayer over the egg and ate it. Needless to say, I survived.

## Assassination

My first trip was interrupted by an event that hit the world's headlines. We had flown from Mumbai to Udaipur to meet Thomas and Mary Matthews, a couple who led a church in the area. But as we were riding in a rickshaw, the driver told us Indira Gandhi had been assassinated by a Sikh. The Indian Government was expecting trouble, and were waiting for people to get to their homes for the evening before making an announcement.

A sinister silence descended over the city and everywhere shut down for 24 hours. People expected tension and bloodshed. I just wanted to keep my head down and stay out of the way. But we prayed and took authority over the situation. I recalled an occasion when there was bloodshed on the streets of Belfast and a group of people prayed that the Lord would bring peace. Following that, a sudden calm descended on the area. It was so significant it was reported on the national news. I felt that, as the people of God, we could speak peace to that part of India and allow God to influence the situation. We heard later that we were in the quietest part of the country.

The next few days were still tense and worrying, though. Around 400 people were killed as Hindus wreaked retribution on Sikhs. Some were decapitated. Many cities imposed a curfew, and we were grateful to God for the way He protected us and led us safely through potentially hazardous situations.

Later on I discovered that the people at the Mission back home were worried about my safety and prayed that God would place a hedge of protection around me. But Olive Peters had other ideas. 'I've put a wall round him, not a hedge. Nothing can get through that wall,' she proclaimed. And nothing did.

Sometime afterwards they asked God to make that wall even higher, so when they heard about assassination and subsequent unrest, they were confident God would protect me. Without the prayer and encouragement of the people at home, our ministries would have had little validity or success.

In the end I arrived safely back home, convinced I would return to that great continent. And eventually I went back with John Norton and his daughter, Victoria, aged ten at the time. She prayed for the money for her fare, and God provided it. And although it eventually became harder for Europeans to stay in India, we were able to visit, and Grace led teams to work among the women – the fulfilment of a personal dream.

## Reflections

India is multi-cultural, multi-faith and multi-almost everything. God certainly used that first trip to enlarge my vision. Every time I went back there, I was moved by the utter poverty and unimaginable living conditions endured by millions, and angered by the enemy's grip on so many lives.

But I was also encouraged by the men and women who gave

sacrificially for the sake of Christ. The country's needs were so great and still are, even though it is more prosperous than it was then. Things are happening. God is doing an amazing work among the Dalits, the outcasts in India's caste system. Hinduism branded them as the lowest of the low, but thousands of them are discovering a real God who exalts the humble and who brings good news to the poor.

My hope and prayer for India remains that the light will overcome the darkness – and the darkness will not be able to withstand it.

# CHAPTER 11

# GREAT WALLS IN CHINA

### Is God's will lost?

Most of us struggle to find God's will. But I'm sure God doesn't want it that way. A friend of mine used to say, 'God's will isn't lost … you don't have to find it!'

In John 10, Jesus told His friends, 'My sheep will know my voice.' He didn't say, 'My sheep will get stressed trying to hear my voice … and when they hear it, they'll struggle to know whether it was me or not.'

A shepherd gives his sheep clear directions. And the sheep recognise his voice – and follow it. It's not complicated.

We are God's sheep, so recognising and following the Shepherd's voice should be straightforward. Other cults and religions cloak their encounters with their gods in mystery. But we can talk to God as a dad, though sadly man-made rituals and mysteries sometimes prevent us from doing that.

God often confirms His will through other people. Sometimes, I believe He has told me something, and then three or four other people tell me the same thing, even though they may not even know each other, and may live hundreds, or even thousands of miles apart. It's exciting when that happens.

God spoke to me like that when He called me to visit China.

During an early visit to America, we went to a church in Russellville, Arkansas, and one of the men said, 'Norman, I have the strongest feeling that God will take you to mainland China. In fact – I see you standing on the Great Wall of China!' Everyone else agreed.

Humanly, this was impossible, as I didn't have any contacts in China. But I responded positively. 'God has done so many other things for me,' I said. 'I believe He will get me to China.'

By the end of that year I was standing on the Great Wall!

## Preparation time

I'd been learning about China for some time. And the more I discovered, the more stirred I became about that vast land. I read about the exploits of the missionaries, how they had supposedly failed and had been expelled during the Cultural Revolution.

I wondered what they had left behind, and what had happened in a country that had locked out the Gospel for 25 years. What kind of Church would I find there, if there was no freedom to preach the Gospel or hold meetings? How many Christians had survived persecution and prison? What percentage of the population was Christian in a country that comprised 35% of the world's population?

I was intrigued. And I soon discovered I wasn't alone. Many Christians were deeply concerned for China. Like me, they were eager to go there. But all we could do was pray. I had a world map covered in pins in my office. It indicated the places I was praying for. China was a priority.

God began to answer our prayers in 1979, with the advent of the liberalisation policy. Stories began to filter through about Christian pastors being released from prison and of millions of people coming to Christ.

I began to believe even more strongly that I would see China one day – and over a period of years, God confirmed this through several other people. The guy in Russellville was one of them. The Shepherd was talking to a sheep called Norman.

## Time to go

In 1985 I met a man called Ross Paterson, who had been a missionary in Taiwan. He had been sent out by the late David Watson's church in York. Ross could speak fluent Mandarin and had been involved in Hong Kong. I said to him, as casually as possible, that if he ever went to China I would like to go with him.

We met again in early 1986 and Ross said to me, 'When are you going to China, Norman?'

'Just give me a date, and I'll go!' I replied, much to his surprise.

'Well, I'm going,' he responded.

'Then I'm coming.' And that was that! Ross asked why I didn't want to pray about accepting the invitation.

'I don't need to!' I told him. 'God's given me a word about it already.'

The trip was arranged for late 1986 and fulfilled another dream. Little did I know the impact God's people there would have on me …

## Our first stop

The plan was to visit Hong Kong, China and Thailand. We went to Hong Kong first. At that time, the Church there was polarised over the charismatic issue – some controversies know no frontiers!

I was deeply moved by some of the people I met, and the incredible work they were doing. David Wang of Asian Outreach was one of the foremost men in Chinese Christian affairs. He had made repeated trips to China and had a lot of contacts. He was a human dynamo and had seen people raised from the dead!

We also met an American named Dennis Balcombe, who led a growing church in Hong Kong. He spoke fluent Chinese and had absorbed the Chinese way of life. He even ate those Chinese 'delicacies' that many Westerners find hard to swallow! His church supplied Christian literature to mainland China.

Jackie Pullinger's work was becoming well known outside Hong Kong through her remarkable book, *Chasing the Dragon*. Her work rehabilitating drug addicts was in transition when we went – former drug addicts and other converts were now taking on responsibility for building the church.

On Sunday afternoons more than 200 gathered for worship and teaching – a cross-cultural, multi-racial meeting if ever there was one. Jackie had managed to blend an astonishing mixture of people into an expression of God's Kingdom. I met former heroin addicts who later became church leaders.

I developed a tremendous admiration for Jackie. Sadly, a number of organisations attempted to take over her work, but she managed to resist their approaches.

In those days, she was still holding Saturday evening meetings in the infamous Walled City. We went along to one of them – I was glad I didn't go alone! It was a hang-out for alcoholics, drug addicts, prostitutes, opium dealers and the notorious triad gangs. Everyone looked at you suspiciously.

The Walled City was like a rabbit warren – a slum area of tenement blocks that housed 60,000 people. The buildings were so close together, they appeared to be joined at the top! And at ground level, a labyrinth of gloomy walkways created dark and dingy tunnels. It was a city within a city.

Our senses reacted to the many strange sights, sounds and smells as we walked down the streets. But one thing was obvious. Jackie was honoured, loved and respected. Everyone else was not so welcome! I was glad I was with her. I don't think I would have lasted long on my own – I was terrified at times.

## Paying the price

Jackie's church met in a small room that had been given to her by local people. Around 60 people were packed in for a meeting, and as Jackie began to speak in fluent Cantonese, the love and presence of God flowed from her. The congregation was a mixture of new converts and people they had brought in from the streets, either drunk or stoned on drugs.

As Jackie led a Bible study, her compassion was obvious and I felt overwhelmed by the love of God. At the end of her talk, she asked people to respond, and six stood to accept Christ. New converts, not long saved themselves, began to pray for them. I broke down and wept like a baby. In fact, I cried so much that the people were concerned and started to pray for me, too! I wanted to ask them not to, for God had touched me. I was completely overwhelmed by His love.

In Hong Kong at that time, you could pay $1,000 a month for a flat.

But God provided Jackie with a better building. The Government gave her a disused refugee camp that comprised 12 Nissen huts, showers, toilets, a canteen, a workshop and a sports area, so her work became even more effective.

The complex became home to an endless stream of homeless people, and Jackie cared for them all, feeding everybody who came. She also had a file on the street sleepers – she looked after them, too. Her shepherd's heart was apparent as she cared for the homeless, drug addicts, displaced people, and down and outs to name but a few. Her love for people was immense.

Jackie showed us her living quarters – a 10ft x 8ft room. That was it. This lady who had been invited to speak all over the world lived in a tiny room. To say that this was challenging, was an understatement.

As I write this in late 2008, Jackie is still faithfully caring for the poor, the unloved and the forgotten, the same as she was when I first met her, more than 20 years ago. Some people wonder why she hasn't moved on to a 'bigger ministry'. But they miss the point. Jesus said the greatest among us would be the servant of all. That's Jackie. How much 'bigger' can you get? She is living proof of how God exalts those who truly humble themselves.

### Slow train to China

In November 1986, I finally made it to mainland China, with Ross Paterson and Rodney Kingston from Worthing. We took the train for the four-hour journey from Hong Kong to Canton and stayed overnight in a hotel called the White Swan. It was unashamedly luxurious for a communist state.

The rooms were probably bugged, and we were closely watched by fearsome ladies stationed on every landing. They checked our comings and goings and monitored who entered and left each room. We were followed both in the hotel and while we were out shopping.

China was an enigma then, and still is now. When we went there, it was starting to liberalise, and on the surface, appeared to be an open society. But beneath, it was strictly controlled. Christians were meant to be accepted, but in reality, they were harassed and persecuted. They couldn't talk openly about the Lord to the Chinese, or even to one another. People were always listening in on their conversations and there was no concept of privacy or private property.

It was different in the recognised state church, called the Three Self Movement. There were some genuine believers there, both in the congregation and leadership. But at the top, it was political and people followed the party line.

There were an estimated 50,000,000 believers in China back then, mainly meeting in small 'house groups'. They were evangelical and often charismatic. That number has grown massively since.

## An Olympic focus

I reflected on that first trip as I watched the Beijing Olympics in summer 2008. In some ways, the country had changed beyond all recognition. Wealth abounded, and China taught the capitalist West a thing or two about putting on a show. But if you scratched the surface, the strict control was still there. It manifested itself several times during the 2008 Olympics, much to the embarrassment of the Chinese Government.

From Canton, we travelled by train to Peking (now Beijing). The train journey lasted 36 hours. There were six people to a compartment, sleeping on three bunks either side, with a 2ft 6in gap between the bunks. By the time you had adjusted your blankets and pillows and found a space for your luggage, there wasn't much room left for your body, especially as the bunks were quite short. Ross, Rodney and I were all at least 6ft tall, and we had plenty of aches and pains by the time we reached our destination.

The regimented Chinese way of life was even obvious on the train. At 10pm, a lady came to switch off the lights. The message was: go to sleep – now! Then she – or one of her colleagues – came back at 6am to wake us up. We weren't given any choice! But the journey was not too bad, although we were relieved when we reached Peking. We hadn't been able to change our clothes for 36 hours!

Peking was just beginning to modernise. Hotels, including the Hilton and Sheraton, were springing up. Since then they've been followed by Starbucks, McDonalds and clothes shops selling designer gear. It's astonishing to see what they have achieved in a few decades.

Interestingly, we never saw those 'traditional' Chinese symbols: the rickshaw and the coolie hat. Everybody wore blue uniforms, except for the military, who wore brown, decorated with red stars. China has the biggest army in the world, comprising between eight to ten million soldiers. They were everywhere, and we had to be careful what we said, since they were all Communist Party members.

## You are either hot or cold …

We stayed in a hostel in Peking where the temperature was the same inside as it was outside – below zero! After our long journey, we wanted a shower, so we made a beeline for the basement. I eagerly turned on the tap – only to be hit by a jet of freezing cold water. 'Oh no,' I muttered. But I was determined not to let it get me down. I prayed out loud, 'I'll bless You for cold water, Lord. I will give You thanks for it. But I'd prefer hot water.' I could hear Ross and Rodney laughing. Suddenly, the water turned hot! I don't remember praising God so loudly, and those 'streams of living hot water' caused some hilarity among my travelling companions.

But worse was to come! One evening, Rodney and I had tummy trouble and needed a toilet – fast! We dashed into the bathroom and were faced with a row of communal toilets. We looked at one another, unsure what to do. But then nature took its course and we didn't have time to consider our dignity! I said to Rodney afterwards, 'Well, I guess we've achieved real fellowship with one another now!'

China's rush towards the 21st century was amazing then – and now it seeks to become a world economic power. Mao Tse-tung was initially blamed for a gigantic step back in Chinese history. People were angry about the Cultural Revolution. Mao was in disgrace after his death and his mausoleum was closed to the public. However, he was later 'upgraded', and his face was on full view to the world during the Olympics.

## Slaughter of the innocents

The modernisation of Chinese society has taken its toll, though. Parents were strongly encouraged to have just one child. The Chinese are besotted with their children and most of these kids are pampered and grossly overweight.

Parents had to pay tax penalties if they had two children, so abortion was common, just as it was in India. Back then, Christians were not really aware of the ethical aspects, and it's still a problem today, though the situation varies from area to area.

We also learned that girls were destroyed, while boys were allowed to live – a truly abominable situation. Boys still predominate, since they can work and earn money. That means that in some areas, baby girls are abandoned, or even murdered at birth. In others, a local official decides whether the baby lives or dies. In some places, women have to undergo forced abortions.

It has been estimated that 15 million baby girls have disappeared since China introduced its one-child-per-family policy in 1979 … figures that must break God's heart. But are we in the United Kingdom any better, with our abortion rates the highest in Western Europe? Although pro-abortion campaigners see a difference between ending the lives of pre-born children and those who have been born, God doesn't.

## The Dying Rooms

Once, when I was in China, I experienced something so terrible, so utterly inhumane, that it will live with me for the rest of my days. I was taken to visit the grim, infamous orphanages that became known as the Dying Rooms. I am still haunted by the images I saw that day.

What are the Dying Rooms? They are also called death camps – places where deformed and disabled children are taken to die. And they are not seriously disabled children – many could have been helped with an operation or proper care.

The orphanage I visited had several floors that were occupied by children who were relatively clean, well fed and properly looked after.

But the Dying Rooms were dreadfully different. Several dozen children, aged between two and 14, lived there and eventually died of neglect. A revolting stench hit me as soon as I walked through the door, and I had to try hard not to vomit.

Children as young as two sat in rows of potty chairs, their wrists and ankles strapped to the sides. There were holes in their seats, with buckets underneath to catch their urine and excrement. Their eyes were dull with hopelessness, their bodies emaciated and shrivelled by malnutrition. They spent the day there, with nothing to do, without stimulation and deprived of love. Then they were lifted out and tied to their beds for the night. Some shared beds with three or four other children in 100 degree temperatures. I saw one little disabled boy who was kept permanently in a room on his own.

And all because they were deformed or disabled. Their parents had abandoned them because they weren't 'normal'. And the Dying Rooms abandoned them to the grave at the rate of several a week.

The Dying Rooms were eventually exposed in a BBC documentary made by Kate Blewett in 1995. The Chinese Government denied they existed, but few could argue with the shocking images captured by the secret video cameras.

Once, when I was speaking at Riverside Church in Nottingham, six Chinese students were furious when I mentioned the Dying Rooms. They emphatically denied they existed – they genuinely believed the allegations were false. But I know what I saw that terrible day.

These images came back to mind during the glitz and glamour of the Beijing Olympics – and especially during the Paralympics. I sympathised with the protestors who claimed that China had no right to host the event when its own recent past was stained with such inhumanity … and where the present situation still gives rise to a host of valid questions.

## On from Peking …

We moved on from Peking to a university, where a lecturer in charge of English studies had asked us to speak. The temperature was still below zero and we found to our dismay that the university heating was not switched on. The 'switch-on' date hadn't arrived – and the actual temperature made no difference. It reminded me of British Rail!

We were given a meal of very clear soup, with tree fungus and cabbage in it. As I sat there, I could see a huge, square polystyrene container filled to the brim with McDonalds junk food floating before my eyes. Sadly it was an illusion – a dream that took a few more weeks to be fulfilled back home in the UK!

We were asked to speak about 'The Relativity of the Christian Religion in England' – we took that as an invitation to share our faith! It was interesting talking to students – they'd been educationally brainwashed. We told them about scientists who believed in God and the Creation, but they didn't believe such people existed. However, Western thinking was beginning to make its mark.

The class comprised three groups – those who had been 'processed' and had not changed; those who were beginning to ask questions; and others who were already opening up to new things. It was easy to tell which students belonged to which group by the questions they asked.

There were also a few believers there, and they asked us leading questions to give us a chance to explain the Gospel. It was a profitable time and a rare chance for someone to speak openly of faith in God in that hostile country.

We left the university and travelled 18 hours by train to Shanghai, an old city that had managed to preserve many of its Chinese traditions. While we were there, we visited the original Willow Pattern Tea House and went to the famous Shanghai River where we saw Chinese junks moored alongside the modern ships. Modernisation had begun …

The English were popular there. You could stand by the river and have a constant stream of people coming up to try out their English. Since then, there has been plenty of work for English teachers. The Chinese are desperate to learn the language, especially as it is now the 'official' Internet vocabulary.

## Making life count

In Shanghai, we met a remarkable man called Pastor Wang Ming-Dao. He had been jailed for 21 years for his faith. We went to visit him in his rooms in a tenement block. We spoke in whispers, afraid of being overheard, but he spoke so loudly the whole block could hear him! He talked about his time in prison, his suffering and his fears. Then he insisted on singing a song to us in English, the old favourite, 'All the way my Saviour leads me'. We were deeply moved … and when he reached the line 'Jesus doeth all things well', I was utterly broken and cried and cried. Such words, coming from a man who had been jailed, beaten and starved for his faith … I just couldn't cope with it.

We asked him to pray for us, but he was so humble, he couldn't understand why. He later went blind and deaf and went to be with the Lord when he was in his nineties. I'm sure he received the special blessing God reserves for those who are persecuted for His sake.

We flew from Shanghai to Canton and met another Pastor called Lin. He had been imprisoned for his faith, too. His wife died five years before his release, so he never saw her again. Can you imagine pain like that?

His years in jail certainly didn't quench his faith – quite the opposite, in fact. Within a few years of being released, he had baptised 900 people! Back then, he reckoned that 2,000 people met in house groups in the city. He had some full-time workers and his church was busy with evangelism and church planting. It's a work that is still growing today.

Pastor Lin had a very high profile and international recognition.

He even had an inscribed pen from President Reagan. He was very outspoken, but was not anti-government – only anti-State church.

He, too, was an inspiration to us and we were deeply moved when we met him. His words remained etched in my memory and are a challenge to all of us … 'I don't know how much time I have. I'm going to make it count!'

## Needs still remain

We left China with a better understanding of where Links could help. Since then, we have funded orphanages, helped import Bibles and have done a lot of work with Jackie Pullinger's team. Our efforts seem like a drop in the ocean compared with the billions of Chinese people. But God calls us to do what we can – and that's what we do.

Now, of course, China is at the forefront of the world economy, has hosted the Olympics and put a man into space. But the spiritual and social needs remain. My fear is the nation may revert to many of its sinister practices now that the Olympics are over.

One of the main needs is for literature. Amity Press produces two million Bibles a year for China. That sounds impressive, until you realise there are 100 million believers there, with thousands of new converts being added every day. You often find there are just one or two Bibles for a whole congregation.

They have a unique way of resolving the problem, though. They cut a Bible up, people take a book each – and learn it, off by heart. Then that person becomes the 'living word' for that chapter in his congregation. So if the pastor wants a reading from Exodus, the 'Exodus' man will stand and recite the appropriate passage. I pity the person who has to learn Isaiah or 2 Chronicles! I'd be happy with 3 John or Jude!

There is also a real need for Bible teaching. When Chinese people get saved, they have no understanding of Scripture – so if someone reads the verse that says, 'If your eye offends you, pluck it out', they may well do just that.

And of course the greatest need in this massive, mysterious land is for prayer. That's something we can all do – and you don't even need a pin in a map to find China.

## Thailand

Next we flew to Thailand and met two members of Team Spirit, Dave Summers and Andy Au. Dave had been a missionary in Thailand for a number of years, but later came back to England to lead a thriving church in Malvern. However, he returned to Thailand with his wife, Carol, and is still working to maintain a fish farm in Chang Mai in the north of the country, in cooperation with Links.

This project enables Dave and Carol to help an unreached people group – the Shan. They are refugees from the ethnic cleansing programme in Burma, and hundreds of them have endured a dangerous trek through the mountains to reach Thailand.

The Thai Government only allows them to stay if they can find work. So the Links project provides them with jobs.

Our time in Bangkok was spent at the Hope of Bangkok Church, led by a Dr Kriengsak. He was a brilliant man with a considerable intellect. He was also a very gifted administrator and no mean theologian.

He originally went to Australia to study Buddhism, but God had other ideas. A Christian witnessed to him, and he came to know Christ as Lord. He joined the Assemblies of God in Australia and led 500 people to the Lord in two years. He then met a Christian

Thai woman in Australia, married her and returned to Bangkok. His life's priority was to preach the Gospel, so he rented a room in a hotel and 17 people came to his first meeting. In five years the congregation grew to 1,600 and needless to say, they soon outgrew that hotel room!

They placed a strong emphasis on prayer. Sundays began with a 7.30am prayer meeting and there were early morning prayer meetings mid-week. Then Sundays were like one of the big British Bible week meetings. It was an incredible set-up – high powered and very successful.

They also ran their own Bible School, their own clinic, had English speaking classes, typing classes, and courses in art and design.

Dr Kriengsak had a vision to plant a church in every district of Thailand by the year 2000 – around 260 churches.

Everybody knew about this vision – it had been successfully passed on to everyone from the youngest convert to the oldest member. It was expressed in every meeting. Everyone knew where they were going and were committed. Dr Kriengsak is now a government advisor, and the church he planted is still flourishing.

During our three days in Thailand we were humbled by the grace of God and people's hard work and single-mindedness. I think the apostle Paul would have felt at home there.

## Lessons to be learned

Our trip to the East made a deep impression on us. There were so many opportunities for people to serve churches and use their jobs as vehicles for preaching the Gospel. And since then scores of people from the West have gone there to do just that. But it's still a difficult and hostile place – the amount of freedom you get varies from day to day. The Chinese people cannot tolerate being embarrassed or losing face – and you can expect a clampdown if that happens.

When we returned home, we knew we had to allow the Holy Spirit to break down our parochial mentality. We feared that the house churches we represented would become spiritually incestuous if they didn't catch a vision for world mission. Many caught it and have real enthusiasm for mission. But it is still the bottom of the agenda in many others, and is the first thing to go when the budget needs cutting. That's sad when you remember that Jesus told us our primary mission is to the poor.

There are unlimited opportunities for people to promote the Kingdom of God on the earth. If only our churches could catch a vision like they did in the Hope of Bangkok!

Links has helped to de-mystify overseas mission, and make it accessible to anyone who wants to get involved. We've helped to take mission out of its cultural box – to pioneer the message that Western churches should empower the poor in other nations, rather than use them to build their own kingdoms.

I long to see dreamers challenged to pursue their dreams and then to dream even bigger ones. There's so much God can do through people who are willing to risk everything for the sake of His Kingdom.

Pastor Lin's words should be our inspiration … 'I don't know how much time I have left. I'm going to make it count!'

# CHAPTER 12

# WHEN GOD
# SAYS NO

### You don't always get what you want

King David had a dream. But he never saw it fulfilled. He wanted to build a wonderful temple for his God. But God said no.

God sent Nathan the prophet to tell David that he had too much blood on his battle-scarred hands to build a place of beauty and majesty. His son, Solomon, would do the job instead.

How do you – how do we – react when God says no to our dreams? It happens. We spent years, dreaming about having children, praying about it, crying about it … but God said no. There have been countries we dreamt of visiting, things we longed to see. But God said no.

There are three options when God gives the dreaded thumbs down to our most deeply-held dreams.

We can either sulk and become disillusioned … and maybe end up walking away, just as the two disciples did on the road to Emmaus when God said no to their dreams of an all-conquering Messiah who would banish the Romans. Plenty of Christians have done the same – they have walked away from their church, from friends, even from their families, because God said no.

Another option is to ignore God, and carry on with our dream regardless. We kid ourselves that a God who gives people their hearts' desires couldn't possibly say no to one of His children. Then we wonder why it all goes wrong. That's what the Israelites did when God refused to let them enter the Promised Land (Numbers 14:44). They went anyway – and met defeat and failure. Leaving the place of blessing usually does.

## The best way

King David gives us the best example of how to cope when God says no. He didn't sulk. Instead, he prepared the people for worship, so that when God's house was complete, they would be ready to fill it with music, dance and praise. Something great came out of David's disappointment. He revolutionised worship, and made it central to the life of the nation.

He appointed 4,000 Levites to look after the musical instruments. He brought in singers, overseen by a chief singer, and trumpet players to blow the trumpets regularly before the Ark of the Covenant. And these men and women weren't just there to make a nice sound with their voices and instruments. They accompanied prophecy and prophesied on their instruments. They sang songs of deliverance – and saw results.

Years later, Nehemiah returned to rebuild Jerusalem after the Israelites had endured the shame of captivity and exile. And when the building work was complete, worship was the top of his agenda. We read in Nehemiah 12:45-46, 'They performed the service of their God and the service of purification, as did also the singers and gatekeepers, according to the commands of David and his son Solomon. For long ago, in the days of David and Asaph, there had been directors for the singers and for the songs of praise and thanksgiving to God'.

David's 'tent' made a lasting impression on Israel's history. But his astonishing accomplishments, that changed earth and touched heaven, resulted from the disappointment when God said no.

Sadly, David's tent didn't last. In Acts 15:16, we read, 'After this I will return and rebuild David's fallen tent'. This refers to the fact that God wanted to restore worship to its rightful place – at the centre of church life. He still does.

Thankfully, we are seeing a revival of worship in our generation. God is raising up men, women and children to lead people into new areas of worship. Gifted song writers are producing songs, hymns and choruses that express God's heart for this moment in history. Many congregations don't just use praise and worship as a prelude to the 'more important' business of listening to the sermon. David's tent is being restored … and you often find that the people who are restoring it are the ones to whom God said no.

## It happened to us

Once when Grace and I went to Texas, we were full of pain because God had said no to us having children. It was hard to come to terms with it. But, as with David, God's 'no' led to a real blessing in worship and praise.

We were aware that some churches in America were restricted in worship. Although they sang, clapped and sang in the Spirit, they lacked other aspects – particularly the prophetic.

We mentioned our concerns to the leaders to see how we could help. It was agreed that we would take a team from back home to do a bit of tent restoring!

So Grace and I took musicians, dancers, a poet and a worship leader over to Texas. We left London with the temperature in the 60s and arrived in Dallas/Fort Worth to find it was 90° plus. It was hot throughout the trip – the thermometer once touched 107°. Thank God for cold drinks and air-conditioning!

Although our hearts were hurting, Grace and I felt a real sense of expectancy and excitement when we arrived. I was thrown in at the deep end by the folks in Azle, our first stop, where I started work at 6.00 in the morning at a prayer breakfast. Who said preachers have an easy life?

Later during our stay, we began to see God move in the meetings. But it was scary stuff! God showed us that we should move out prophetically by using music and dance. This was new to us, but we risked it, and God honoured us. We called people out, prophesied and played music to them and then danced out the prophecy. Again and again, God confirmed His word and at times the clarity of the words of knowledge and ministry were quite astounding. Music and dance brought a new dimension to God's voice.

One man in his early 40s joined the drama team. He was a tall, well-built man, every inch a Texan, with jeans, boots and Texan belt. I wondered what he was going to do! But I was thrilled when I saw him acting out what God had showed him. He told me later that he'd wanted to dance in church since he was 17, but had never found the opportunity.

We realised that our narrow thinking had robbed people of legitimate ways of expressing their love for God and of bringing God's word to us. Amid our pain, the Lord showed us that dance, music and drama originated with Him. It belongs to His Church. The world has stolen what was rightfully ours. As I shared this, many people realised that being creative did not mean being worldly.

## Confronting tradition

It was a real delight to see children eager to stay in the meeting so they could dance, worship and bless the Lord. They usually couldn't get out fast enough! Many of the families wept at what God was doing among their children.

Our poetry, dancing, music and drama brought an enthusiastic response in Texas, and our final evening lasted four hours. At the end, everyone wept together. Our team had been loved, cared for and spoilt, and was reluctant to leave. But we had other places to go.

One pastor in a town near Dallas was strongly against the way we were portraying dance. But his doubts disappeared when he saw one of our women dance. Her movements reflected what was going on in his life and God spoke to him clearly.

It was a different atmosphere in Houston, but God did some precious things among us. People began to realise it was acceptable to laugh, cry, stand, kneel, be still, dance, make a noise or be quiet in God's presence. We were simply reclaiming what the devil had stolen from us, and many people were blessed.

We left Houston to travel to Laredo, where we met our good friends, Norman and Sandra Howell, who pastored the Church of the Crossroads.

Their church included a number of Hispanics, and it was hard to understand why they found it a problem to get involved in dance – after all, it was so strong in their culture. But I realised that many of them were middle-class, and were trying to forget their historical Mexican roots.

On the Sunday morning, we performed a play called *Superfaith*, and then Grace gave an appeal. Thirty people came to the front, prostrated themselves in the presence of God and wept. It was a moving occasion – people were touched by the Holy Spirit and families were blessed.

And it didn't end there. Everyone got out of their seats and danced together for the first time in the church's history! Then at our last meeting we broke bread in a different way. Again the Holy Spirit moved. People were reconciled and expressed their love and commitment to one another. And the blend of different styles of music showed how many ways we had to express our love for God and one another. The musicians moved from classical to country, to worship, with no gaps in between. There was no sense of 'this is sacred music and this is secular'.

On our last evening we crossed the border into Mexico to enjoy a real Mexican meal, complete with traditional players and singers who were *not* trying to forget their roots! But the contrast between Mexico and the USA was vivid – a sobering reminder that two-thirds of the planet lived like Mexicans and not like their affluent neighbours.

Our last destination was Dallas. By the time we arrived we were pretty jaded, and the meeting was difficult after a long journey. But we saw God break in, especially among the young people. We were weak – worn out in fact. But He was strong!

We left with many memories of lives that had been touched and changed – ours especially. We'd been to new places with God in praise and worship. We'd also learned a lot about swimming pools, hamburgers, cowboy hats, belts and boots, good friendships and the ups and downs of operating as a fairly large team. We all came back with a fresh vision and new dreams. Seeing God fulfil one dream inspires you to believe for others.

But it happened because God said no.

# CHAPTER 13

# THE LAST CHAPTER?

### Take it easy? No chance!

It would be very tempting for Grace and me to sit back and think, 'It's time to take it easy.' Thankfully, we are not like that. We are both still dreaming of new things to do, new projects to accomplish, and new ways to serve the Lord.

This book first came out back in 1988. It was called *God Gave Me a Dream* then. We can remember the day we finished it really well.

Wimbledon had just beaten mighty Liverpool in the FA Cup Final – and there I was, dictating my words of wisdom into a microphone linked to a tape recorder, ready for my friend, Rod Boreham, to type it up on his old Olivetti typewriter.

It's laptops and digital recording devices these days. But some things haven't changed. At the end of that original book, I said, 'We're not satisfied.' We're still not!

We finished the first version with many dreams unfulfilled.

Since then, some of them have come to pass – sometimes in ways that we could never have imagined, and occasionally in ways we didn't particularly like! God has surprised us, time and time again.

Other dreams are still being fulfilled in the lives of our many spiritual sons and daughters. And if you believe in generational blessings as we do, then it is not difficult to see how some wonderful things are going to happen, long after we've gone to glory.

This concept has really helped us as we've slowed down because of the advancing years! Recently, I've said no to invitations to Peru and Mongolia, and those refusals cost me something. You always want to make one more trip, especially to somewhere new, or somewhere you've dreamed about. It left me feeling sad.

I confided in Richard Hubbard, the new Links director, who has taken on the mantle from Grace and me. His reply really helped me.

'But, Norman, you *did* go. Your spiritual sons and daughters went. They took your dream in their hearts ... a dream that's still multiplying in the hearts of hundreds, maybe thousands of people worldwide.' Those remarks really blessed me – the idea of others carrying the torch for us satisfies us as much as going ourselves.

I've just reached retirement age, but I'm still dreaming. And so's Grace – and she's older than I am! Why? Because if we don't have dreams, there's no point in living.

We still have more things we'd like to see, and I guess that we always will. Fulfilling our destiny is so important to us, even as we grow older. And of course, the enemy knows that dreamers can cause serious damage to him and his kingdom.

Someone once said to us, 'Thank you for modelling growing old.' We must confess that we were a bit taken aback at first! But they followed it up with these words: 'You have both maintained your enthusiasm, vision, passion and longing for the lost, the poor and the marginalised – and you are still breaking new ground.'

That means a lot to us – especially on those days when we feel a bit tired and our joints ache! But I guess that is our longing – to keep dreaming, to keep trusting God.

## Finishing well

One man put it this way: 'It is not how you start that matters – it is how you finish.' We're not quite finished yet. But we're going to keep on dreaming while we can!

When I think back to those prayer meetings in the Dagenham Elim Church, I realise that God has brought us a long way. The dreams Grace and I had in our hearts to reach the world were not illusions. The Holy Spirit placed them there, and we have seen many of them come true. But we are not satisfied. Grace and I both feel excited about the future. God is the God of new things and we believe the best is yet to come.

## Keeping going

Someone once asked us, 'How do you keep going?' We sometimes ask ourselves the same question. But let me tell you a story that helps to answer it.

Back in 1988, I was asked to see a lady called Shirley Chapman. She worked for Wycliffe Bible Translators in the Amazon jungle, and was home on furlough. I arranged for her to come to lunch with us, to give her a bit of encouragement – she only lived about 15 minutes away in Goodmayes, Essex.

She arrived around 12.30pm and left at midnight! Her story was both humbling and inspiring.

She had spent 30 years working among the Paumari tribe in the massive Amazon jungle. She and a colleague, a lady called Meinki Slazenger, had given up their careers and the comforts of the Western world to go and live among this group of 800 people. She laid down her life to bring them health and education. She taught them to read and write. She learned their language and became the first person to write it down on paper.

She also translated the New Testament into the Paumari language. We've got a copy of it in our flat – it's one of our most precious possessions.

I asked Shirley, who was in her 50s then, if we could support her. But she refused. Then I asked if we could visit her. And she agreed.

That visit changed Grace and me. We saw the love of Jesus being expressed to this undiscovered group of Indians … we saw the great commission being fulfilled before our eyes … 'making disciples of all nations …'

Shirley and Meinki lived in a house on stilts in the jungle, next to the Purus river, hundreds of miles from civilisation. They had no electricity, no running water and very few possessions. Their living conditions were basic. While we were there, we ate monkey, turtle and sea cow.

These two incredible women had also started a church among the Paumaris. Between 80 to 100 people attended. That's ten per cent of the population – a revival by any standard. We talk about church planting. But these ladies were doing it. Shirley's retired now.

Shirley and Meinki are living examples of following a dream. They are ordinary folk, just like us. But they are God's unsung heroes, affecting people's lives through their sacrifice and extending God's Kingdom on the earth. They forfeited their own lives, and careers, and missed the chance to get married and have children. They had no platform, no recognition, and no glory. Just a life of servanthood.

Imagine if Shirley and Meinki could be multiplied, hundreds of times over, across the world. Imagine the impact. Imagine the millions of lives that would be changed, imagine …

… There we go, dreaming again! We're up for it. Are you?